THE PENGUIN CLASSICS

EDITED BY E. V. RIEU

L 8

VIRGIL
THE PASTORAL POEMS

A TRANSLATION OF THE ECLOGUES

BY E. V. RIEU

PENGUIN BOOKS

HARMONDSWORTH · MIDDLESEX

THIS TRANSLATION,
SPECIALLY MADE FOR PENGUIN BOOKS LTD, WAS
FIRST PUBLISHED IN 1949

MADE AND PRINTED IN GREAT BRITAIN
FOR PENGUIN BOOKS LTD
BY HUNT, BARNARD AND CO. LTD

CONTENTS

A*

INTRODUCTION

1

THE aim of this translation of Virgil's Pastoral Poems, the *Eclogues* (or *Select Pieces*), as they are usually called, is to introduce new readers to the unknown delights of Latin poetry. These poems were the first that Virgil published in book form. They have a strong individuality of their own, which has remained fresh and unimpaired through twenty centuries of false and true appreciation. Yet, like all the most significant works of art, they are largely representative of their period too. No happier entry could be found to the golden age of Roman letters.

Of the man who wrote them, apart from what he himself reveals, we know only too little – more than of Homer or Shakespeare, rather less than of Chaucer, much less than of Milton. This is so true that controversial statements cannot be excluded even from the briefest outline of his life.

Publius Vergilius Maro (to give him his full Latin name and spell it correctly) was born in 70 B.C. at the village of Andes, which lay not very far, though its exact location is disputed, from the small town of Mantua, in that part of Northern Italy which was called Cisalpine Gaul. His people may be described as yeoman stock. His father, who combined farming with bee-keeping on a commercial scale, had the resources and the foresight to give him a sound schooling, at Cremona first, and later at Milan. He was even prosperous enough to send his son to Rome, at the age of seventeen, to complete his education and prepare for a career. Virgil's university training, as we should now call it, began with a course of rhetoric. But the elder Virgil had misjudged the shy and sensitive genius of his son, who discovered, after a maiden speech in court, that he was not cut out for success in politics or at the bar. After this false start, Virgil turned to philosophy, with an enthusiasm that he has himself described for us in a charming little poem, and sat, for some years, it seems, at the feet of the Epicurean lecturer, Siro, in Naples. Siro was popular with the rich and ambitious youth of the day, and it was at this time that Virgil formed those friendships with the future leaders of political and intellectual life that we hear of in the *Eclogues*. He had already tried his hand at verse – we have several of his early efforts[1] – but he had not found himself yet; and there is good reason for believing that the impulse which produced the *Eclogues* was the outcome of this prolonged period of philosophic study and of the literary contacts it afforded.

In embracing philosophy, Virgil had begged the Muse of poetry not to abandon him altogether, but to make her visits 'rare and seemly'. She took him at his word. He was a slow worker, and years passed before the *Eclogues* took shape. In fact, though written at odd times in his third decade, the collection was not published till Virgil was thirty-one, in the year 39 B.C., by which time his friend Cornelius Gallus, a younger member of the literary coterie I have referred to, already had several well-established volumes of verse to his credit. There is something very characteristic of Virgil's diffident and late-maturing genius in this delay. Moreover, he was an awkward and shy, though

---

1. Many, at any rate, of the short poems in the collection entitled *Catalepton* are now considered to be genuine by competent authorities.

attractive, young man. One can almost believe that he would not have published at all, had the friends who already knew his poems not forced him to do so, and that no rising poet was ever so embarrassed by the popular success that his work achieved. For it seems to have taken Rome by storm. The *Eclogues* were even recited or sung in the theatre – by no means a regular by-product, in those days, of publication in book form – and their author received such acclamations as were generally reserved for the ruler of the Roman world.

His reputation was now established. He became, if not the 'court poet' of the early Empire (for he preserved his integrity to the very end), the poet most esteemed at court. Octavian's minister, Maecenas, encouraged him in the production of his next work, the *Georgics*, over which he toiled for seven years, living for the most part in Southern Italy; and, when this was done, Octavian himself fostered and cherished in all the slow stages of its growth the still greater work which occupied his last decade. He died (19 B.C.) in his fifty-first year, and the *Aeneid*, which he had ordered to be burnt, was published in its unfinished form by his literary executors, at the Emperor's command.

II

Before returning to the *Eclogues* it will be well to glance at the history of Virgil's day, although the direct references which he makes to contemporary events are scarcely more numerous than those which Jane Austen makes in her novels to the Napoleonic Wars. When he first saw the reeds of Mincius and the foot-hills of the

Alps, the aristocratic regime in Italy, which we call the
Republic, was already tottering to its fall, and, during
the whole of his second decade, Julius Caesar, who
was destined to destroy it, was engaged on those cam-
paigns in Gaul which enabled him eventually to cross
the Rubicon with a devoted force and make his decisive
march on Rome (49 B.C.). The civil wars that followed
his seizure of power were renewed rather than termin-
ated by his assassination five years later, when Virgil
was twenty-six; and it took Octavian, the young
grandnephew whom Julius had adopted as his son and
successor, thirteen years to overcome, first his father's
murderers, and then his own associate and rival,
Antony. The battle of Actium (31 B.C.) settled Antony's
fate, and brought peace, with despotism, to the Roman
world. Octavian finally established himself as 'Princeps'
in 27 B.C., took the title of Augustus, and under that
name is known to us as the first emperor of Rome.

To these catastrophic events, Virgil (though there
is a story that in spite of his poor health he fought in
one campaign) reacted rather as a poet and a thinker
than as a politician or a partisan. It is true that he
admired Julius Caesar – as a boy he may well have
seen and been captivated by the great proconsul when
he wintered in Cisalpine Gaul – and that he afterwards
followed the rising star of Octavian, whom he is supposed to have met first in his early years at Rome; but
if he worships his heroes, it is not as conquerors, nor
even as men, but rather as the divinely directed forces
that brought discipline and happiness to a distracted
world. Of war itself he speaks with horror. Twice in
the *Eclogues* he repudiates its claims upon a pen which
is otherwise and better engaged. In the *Georgics* he says,

'Give me the woodlands and the brooks, and let the glory go'. The *Aeneid* itself is a tribute to Rome, not as a destructive, but as a civilizing power.

III

But I digressed from the *Eclogues* at the moment of their publication and their triumph. What is there in them that assured their immediate and their lasting success? It must certainly be some quality that transcends all differences of idiom, time and place. And it is evidently something subtle and difficult to define, for the answers to the question have been almost as many as the readers of these much-loved poems. Virgil's friend Horace summed up contemporary opinion when he said that they had caught 'the tender and playful spirit of the Muse whom rural scenes delight'[1] – an excellent comment, though only part of the truth. Our own poets – Spenser, Milton, Pope, Tennyson – when they drank at their source, found other qualities in the *Eclogues* than this. Yet it must be admitted that in the long run it was the tendency of imitators to emphasize the apparent artificiality of the original. In the 19th century it was possible for serious critics to speak of the *Eclogues* as though they were as spurious as the Watteau shepherdesses whose distant ancestors they are. John Conington, for instance, stressing and misinterpreting Virgil's debt to the Greek pastoral poet Theocritus, grants him some felicity of style, but condemns his whole work as 'unreal', as 'palpable and

1. This translation of *molle atque facetum* is what a close study of the *Eclogues* has suggested to me. I am well aware that there are other interpretations.

avowed imitation', and even as a 'corruption' of literature. And though, among Conington's contemporaries, the *Eclogues* found other and less censorious devotees, I suspect that with many of them it was their prettiness rather than their depth that counted. It was left to the 20th-century critics to rediscover their excellence, and they did their work almost too well, for the diversity of their findings, though a tribute to Virgil's many-sided genius, is perplexing. Tenney Frank, in his important biography of the poet, cleared away many ancient misinterpretations on allegorical lines, brought Virgil and his times to life, and presented the *Eclogues* as a sincere and sympathetic study of the pastoral life of the day. E. K. Rand, in an equally illuminating study, *The Magical Art of Virgil*, showed us the poet working his way through the pastoral to the epic form, and brought out the element of hero-worship that figures in the work. Meanwhile J. S. Phillimore, in his *Pastoral and Allegory*, had put new life into the allegorical view of the poems, emphasizing Virgil's importance in the circle of young writers within which he worked, and leaving us to regard each Eclogue as bearing direct reference to the lost work of some other member of this coterie. Finally, the most recent translator of Virgil makes a new and surprising departure down the old cul-de-sac by dismissing the *Eclogues* as the immature and artificial experiments of a youthful poet.

The poems have many facets, and there is truth in nearly all these views – even in Conington's. Virgil did present the Greek idyl to the Latin world: he was the Roman Theocritus. Yet at the same time his pastoral sketches were not out-of-date nor purely fanciful: they were closely related to the peasants' experiences in a time of strife and disorder. Again, still anchoring himself to external realities, he did seize occasions to praise the great men of the day. And those scholars too are right who suggest that, if we had the poems of Gallus and Virgil's other friends in our hands, we should find a wealth of subtle allusion, even of parody, in his work.

But I am left with the feeling that Virgil not only could, but did, achieve all these aims, and something else as well; that they conditioned the form his writing took, but did not inspire it. Behind them all, I detect an overriding poetic impulse, which persists through the diversity of all ten pieces, justified Virgil in making one book of them, accounts for their early success, and – still more important from our point of view – explains the fact that 20th-century people who know little of the politics and literature of Virgil's times, and care less, can still succumb to their enchantment.

If then I must embark on my own interpretation, I should say that what inspired and unifies the *Eclogues* is a poet's perception of certain realities that underlie our relation to the world around us. It was in his Arcady, the pastoral world of his memories and of his fancy, that Virgil found the window which gave him this vision of the truth, and sensed the spirit that pulsates in everything that is, and makes a harmony of man, tree, beast and rock. Nature is fundamentally at one with man, though towns and politics and war make him a refugee from her and from the truth. It is the shepherd and his sheep that are her nurslings and her confidants. It is they who comprehend, when the 'woods on Maenalus make music and the pine-trees speak'. Virgil had listened with them as a boy, and he

remembers and reports what he had heard and seen –
a world where everything is quick with understanding,
where 'the rocks burst into song and the plantations
speak'; where brooks are checked and lynxes overcome
by the music of the reeds aroused from their native
indolence by Pan; where the pipe itself instructs the
player; where the tamarisk sheds tears for the unhappy
lover, and sympathetic sheep stand round him in their
grief, while the truant Nymphs who fail to rally to his
side are chidden for remissness in their task.

It is easy to dismiss these personifications and
pathetic fallacies as the pretty conceits that a Roman
poet took over from the teeming world of Greek fancy.
But I think it would be wrong. It is at such points that
Virgil adds significance to beauty, contacts reality
most closely, and expresses his vision and his very self
most clearly. It is here that he is most tender and most
playful. He invites us to enjoy these touches, not as
meretricious adornments, but because they are open-
ings on an unseen and delightful world. The truth he
saw is not only a solemn awe-compelling thing, but
something that can pierce the trees and rocks with
ecstasy, and also make a poet smile. It is an outlook on
the world which more than one modern philosophy
might not repudiate, even if it failed to recognize the
idiom in which Virgil spoke.

I submit then that, through all their diversity and the
multitude of subordinate meanings that are rightly
found in them, the *Eclogues* are symphonic variations
on this elusive theme. Wordsworth had comparable
intuitions, which he reports more fully and in other
terms. Housman too, when he walked by Onny, Teme
and Clun, saw an Arcady of his own, very different

from Virgil's, and with sterner laws in it and sadder men. Virgil himself, when he wrote the *Georgics* in his middle years, developed a different, though parallel, interpretation of man's place in nature. But the *Georgics* are another story. All I have done here is to express sincerely, if inadequately, what one of its lovers finds in Virgil's earliest work.

IV

But the analysis of poetry is apt to defeat its own purpose, and the reader may well ask why, having already given him hints of what I hope he may find in the poems themselves, I should have thought it necessary to comment on them in the series of ten Essays that I have added to this book. Let me tell him at once that, though I could not resist the temptation of writing these, he is under no obligation to read them. If he does so, in spite of this reprieve, he will find that I have attempted, not further explanations of the spirit of the *Eclogues*, but some discussion of the *form* that spirit took, with comments on points of interest in their setting and their history, and a little more information about Virgil's life and times – in fact a not too serious introduction into the fascinating field of Virgilian studies. Any scholar who may happen to pick up this book will readily acquit me of having made anything like a thorough analysis of the difficulties involved. Indeed he is more likely to feel that I have been too light-hearted. But I maintain that we have Virgil's own authority not to take him with too great solemnity. He speaks of his book as a prank he had allowed himself in the audacity of youth. Besides, there are many

points in the long history of Virgilian scholarship
where it is impossible to restrain a smile.

Some of my indebtedness to previous students I
have already implied. The remainder will become even
more apparent in the Essays. I will confine myself here
to a word on the earliest and perhaps the greatest of
them all, the 4th-century scholar, or scholars, whose
multiple personality I refer to for the sake of con-
venience under the single name of Servius. Servius
may find more allegories in Virgil than we care to
endorse, but he is right in his estimate of the varieties
of meaning that are to be sought in his words. He is
learned, acute, and full of good things. He knows his
Virgil inside out, and if I sometimes venture to make
fun of him, it is with the uneasy feeling that the last
laugh may rest with him.

In order to avoid footnotes to the poems, I have
discussed in the Essays a few points on which the
modern reader may be glad of enlightenment. Others,
and in particular the unfamiliar names from ancient
geography and Greek legend, I have dealt with by
devoting a few words to each in a Glossary at the end
of the book. Reference to that index is no more essen-
tial to the enjoyment of the *Eclogues* than is a reading
of the Essays.

Of the translation itself I will only say that it might
well have been less like Virgil if I had laboured to
render the music of his hexameters in some traditional
form of English verse. I have seen no attempt of the
kind that has not lost more than it has gained by
squeezing Virgil into a mould of alien design.

For many an incisive comment and shrewd suggestion made when this book was in the typescript

stage, I am deeply indebted to that seasoned Virgilian scholar, Mr W. F. Jackson Knight. He is not to be held responsible for anything I finally wrote, but without his generous help the work would have been far more faulty than it is. I should be glad to think that the zeal he devoted to *The Pastoral Poems* may stimulate him to produce that new edition of the *Eclogues* which is so much needed to-day.

The drawing on the title-page is from the Roman salver, called the Neptune Plate, which was recently discovered at Mildenhall and is now displayed in the British Museum. Though the instrument which the young man is playing is not, I think, one of those referred to by Virgil, the artist might almost have had the Eighth Eclogue in mind. The picture of Pan on the cover is also taken from the Neptune Plate.

Highgate, Feb. 1947   E. V. R.

I

THE DISPOSSESSED

Meliboeus
Tityrus

Meliboeus. Tityrus, while you lie there at ease under the awning of a spreading beech and practise country songs on a light shepherd's pipe, I have to bid good-bye to the home fields and the ploughlands that I love. Exile for me, Tityrus – and you lie sprawling in the shade, teaching the woods to echo back the charms of Amaryllis.

Tityrus. Ah Meliboeus, the man to whom I owe this happy leisure is a god. Yes, I shall always treat him as a god. He shall have an altar, and I will often stain it with the blood of a young lamb from my fold. See for yourself. He gave the word – and my cattle browse at large, while I myself can play the tunes I fancy on my rustic flute.

Meliboeus. Don't think that I am jealous. *My* only feeling is amazement – with every farm in the whole countryside in such a state of chaos. Look at myself, unfit for the road, yet forced to drive my goats on this unending trek. See, Tityrus, I can hardly drag this one along. Just now, in the hazel thicket here, she bore two kids – I had been counting on them – and had to leave the poor things on the naked flints. Ah, if I had not been so blind, I might have known that we were in for this disaster. Often enough I had been warned by Heaven, when lightning struck the oaks.

But tell me, Tityrus, who is this god of yours?

Tityrus. I was a simpleton, Meliboeus. I used to think that the city they call Rome was like our market-town, where we shepherds are accustomed to drive down our new-weaned lambs. Arguing from what I knew, from a dog's likeness to a puppy and a goat's to her kids, I measured big by little things. But I soon saw that Rome stands out above all other cities as the cypress soars above the drooping undergrowth.

Meliboeus. And what was the urgent business that took you to Rome?

Tityrus. The call of liberty. I had been lazy; and freedom beckoned to me late – not till the hairs that fell as I clipped my beard began to show a touch of grey. However, the call did come; and after those long years I answered it, when Galatea had thrown me over and Amaryllis had my heart. For I confess that in Galatea's day I entertained no hope of getting free nor cared to save my pence. It made no odds how often a lamb from my fold was chosen for sacrifice, nor what rich cheeses pressed in my dairy went to the thankless town: I never came home with a pocketful of coin.

Meliboeus. Ah, Amaryllis, now I know why you were putting up such wistful prayers and for whose sake you left the apples hanging on the trees! Tityrus had gone. Why, Tityrus, the very pines and springs, the very vineyards here, have sighed for you.

Tityrus. What was a man to do? There was nowhere else than Rome where I could bring my serfdom to an end or find a god so able to protect me. It was there, Meliboeus, that I saw the young man for whom my altar is going to smoke on twelve days in the year. There too that I had from him the first kind answer to my suit. 'Lads,' he said, 'let your cattle graze, as you have always done, and put your bulls to stud.'

Meliboeus. Happy old man! So your land will still be yours. And it's enough for you, even though the bare rock and the marshland with its mud and reeds encroach on all your pastures. Your pregnant ewes will never be upset by unaccustomed fodder; no harm will come to them through meeting other people's flocks.

Happy old man! You will stay here, between the rivers that you know so well, by springs that have their Nymphs, and find some cool spot underneath the trees. Time and again, as it has always done, the hedge there, leading from your neighbour's land, will have its willow-blossom rifled by Hyblaean bees and coax you with a gentle humming through the gates of sleep. On the other side, at the foot of the high rock, you will have the vine-dresser singing to the breezes, while all the time your dear full-throated pigeons will be heard, and the turtle-dove high in the elm will never bring her cooing to an end.

Tityrus. And so I say, stags must take wing and feed in the upper air; the sea roll back and leave her fishes high and dry; nations go wandering across each other's lands, and Germans drink in exile from the Tigris, or Parthians from the Saone – before the memory of my patron's gracious look could vanish from my heart.

Meliboeus. Yes, but meanwhile the rest of us are off; some to foregather with the Africans and share their thirst; others to Scythia, and out to where the Oxus rolls the chalk along; others to join the Britons, cut off as they are by the whole width of the world. Ah, will the day come, after many years, when I shall see a place that I can call my home, see turf piled high on my poor cottage roof, and in due time survey with pride the modest crop that is my little realm?

Is some blaspheming soldier to own these acres I have broken up and tilled so well – a foreigner to reap these splendid fields of corn? Look at the misery to which we have sunk since Romans took to fighting one

another. To think that *we* have sown for men like that
to reap! Yes, Meliboeus, now graft your pears; now
plant a row of vines!

Forward, my goats; forward, the flock that used to
be my pride. Never again, stretched out in some green
hollow, shall I spy you far away, dangling on the rocky
hillside where the brambles grow. There will be no
songs from me, my goats, and I shall lead you no more
to crop the flowering clover and the bitter willow
shoots.

Tityrus. Yet surely you could sleep here as my guest
for this one night, with green leaves for your bed? I
have got ripe apples, and some mealy chestnuts and a
good supply of cheese. See over there – the rooftops of
the farms are already putting up their evening smoke
and shadows of the mountain crests are falling farther
out.

II

THE PASSIONATE SHEPHERD
TO HIS LOVE

THE PASSIONATE SHEPHERD
TO HIS LOVE

THE shepherd Corydon had lost his heart to the beautiful Alexis. But Alexis was his master's favourite. There was no hope for Corydon. His only comfort was to haunt the spots where the high beeches spread unbroken shade, and there, alone in idle ecstasies of love, he made the mountains and the woodlands listen to these disordered shreds of song:

'Cruel Alexis, do you care nothing for my songs? Have you no pity for me? You will end by driving me to death.

'This is the hour when even cattle seek the coolness of the shade; when even the green lizard lies hidden in the thorny brake; when Thestylis brews a fragrant soup of pounded garlic and wild-thyme for the reapers wearied by the scorching heat. Yet I am wandering in the paths that you have trod, under the burning sun, while the orchards echo to the harsh cicadas' notes and mine.

'Would it not have been better to put up with the sulky moods of Amaryllis and the airs she gives herself? Or with Menalcas, dark though he is – and you so fair?

'Beautiful boy, do not rely too much on lovely colouring. The white flower of the privet falls: black bilberries are picked.

'Alexis, you despise me. You do not even ask what sort of man I am, what flocks I may possess, how rich I am in snowy milk. Yet a thousand lambs of mine range the Sicilian hills; summer and winter I have fresh milk in plenty.

'And I can sing, as once upon a time Theban

Amphion used to sing when he was calling home the cows on Attic Aracynthus.

'Nor am I as ill-favoured as all that. Down by the sea the other day, I saw myself reflected when the dying wind had left the water calm. You could compare me even with Daphnis, and I should have no fears – if mirrors do not lie.

'If only you could bring yourself to live with me under some humble roof in the homely countryside, to shoot the stag, and drive a herd of goats with a green marsh-mallow switch!

'With me beside you in the woods you will learn to sing like Pan. Pan taught us how to join a set of reeds with wax. Pan cares for sheep and for the people who look after them.

'Nor let it vex you when you chafe your lip on a reed. Amyntas shrank from nothing – he was so keen to learn the secrets of the art.

'I have a pipe made of seven hemlock stalks of graded length. Damoetas, long ago, as he lay dying, made me a present of it. "You are its second slave," he said to me. That's what Damoetas said; and Amyntas, like the fool he is, was jealous.

'Another thing – I found two little chamois in a valley where a man might come to grief. They have kept the white spots on their coats and twice a day they suck the same ewe dry. I am saving them for you, though Thestylis has long been pestering me to let her have them.

'And so I shall, since you turn up your nose at all my gifts.

'Ah, lovely youth, come here. Can you not see the Nymphs, laden with baskets full of lilies, all for you?

See the white Naiad, plucking, for you, pale irises and poppy-heads, binding narcissus to the fragrant anise-flower, with cassia and other scented herbs twined in, and flaming marigolds to make the modest blueberries look their best.

'Myself I'll pick you quinces with their white and tender bloom, and the chestnuts Amaryllis loved when she was mine. And waxen plums. Yes; let the plum be honoured too.

'And I'll take toll of you as well, you laurels, and your friends the myrtles. Set side by side you blend your perfumes very sweetly.

'Corydon, you're a clown. Alexis has no use for gifts. And if you try to win him in that way, Iollas will outbid you.

'Oh misery! What have I brought on my unhappy self? My wits are gone: I have let the south wind dash my flowers, and had the wild-boars paddling in the clear water of my springs.

'Foolish Alexis, why should you run from a country-man like me? There have been gods who made the woods their home. And so did Paris, Prince of Troy. Pallas can stay inside the citadels she builds for towns. I ask for nothing better in the whole world than the woods.

'The wild-eyed lioness pursues the wolf; the wolf pursues the kid; the kid herself goes gambolling in search of flowering clover. And I chase you. Each is drawn on by what delights him most.

'I see the oxen pulling home the ploughs – their yokes are set to lift the shares. And now the westering sun has doubled every shadow's length. But love still burns me up – and what can stop it?

'Corydon, Corydon, what is this madness that has got you down? You have left your vines half-pruned and the elms they grow on thick with leaves. Rather than this, why not get busy on a useful piece of work and plait a basket with some osier-twigs or pliant reeds? If this Alexis treats you with contempt, you'll find another.'

III

ARE THESE MELIBOEUS' SHEEP?

Menalcas
Damoetas
Palaemon

Menalcas. Whose flock is that, Damoetas? Tell me, are these Meliboeus' sheep?

Damoetas. No; they are Aegon's. Aegon has just left me in charge of them.

Menalcas. Poor sheep, unlucky all the time! Aegon runs off to keep Neaera warm, fearing she may prefer me to himself, while here a hireling shepherd milks his ewes every half hour, till the whole flock is dry and the lambs are left without a drop.

Damoetas. Think twice before you bring that up against a man. I know what *you* did, and the shrine you did it in. You made the very he-goats look askance. The Nymphs are tolerant: they only laughed.

Menalcas. Just as they did, of course, when they saw me with a hook slashing at Micon's growing vines and vineyard trees!

Damoetas. Or here by the old beeches when you smashed up Daphnis' bow and arrows, like the blackguard that you are. Why, you were in torment from the moment when you saw them given to the boy, and would have died if you hadn't managed to indulge your spite.

Menalcas. What can the farmers do, when thieves become so bold? Did I not see you sneaking up to cut off one of Damon's goats? And when his mongrel barked and I called out, 'Tityrus, what is that villain after now? Better round up your flock!' there you were, skulking in the rushes.

Damoetas. Hadn't I beaten Damon in a match? Hadn't my pipe and singing won me a goat from him? Why shouldn't he pay up? You may not know it, but that goat was mine. Damon himself admitted it to me, but said he could not pay.

Menalcas. You beat him in a match? I don't believe you ever owned a set of reed-pipes joined with wax. All you were good for was to stand at the cross-roads and scrape a miserable tune out of one squeaking straw.

Damoetas. Right! Will you make a match of it and see what each of us can do, singing in turn? I stake this heifer. Don't turn up your nose: she comes to the milk-pail twice a day and suckles a pair of calves as well. It's your turn now to name your stake.

Menalcas. I'm not like you: I dare not gamble on a beast. I have a father and a spiteful step-mother at home. Twice every day both count the flock, and one of them counts the kids as well. No; since you are so set on this mad game, I name a stake which even you will grant is far more valuable — a pair of beechwood cups carved by the great Alcimedon himself. Embossed on each by his unerring knife there is a pliant vine, wreathing its scattered clusters with pale ivy. There are two figures in between: one is of Conon, one of — who was the other sage who mapped the whole celestial sphere for mankind with his rod, and fixed the dates when we should reap or should bend our shoulders to the plough? I have not yet touched them with my lips: I keep them stowed away.

Damoetas. That same Alcimedon made a pair of cups for me as well as you. He draped the handles with soft acanthus leaves, and in between put Orpheus and the trees coming after him. 'I have not yet touched them with my lips: I keep them stowed away!' One look at the heifer, and you'll say no more about the cups.

Menalcas. I swear that you shall not escape me now.
I am ready to meet you on whatever terms you choose.
But we must have a judge ... Why, here's Palaemon.
He will do. I am going to see that from to-day you
never challenge anyone again.

Damoetas. All right, begin, if you have anything
to sing. I shall not keep you waiting. I am not going to
run away from any judge. I only beg Palaemon, our
good neighbour here, to listen to our songs with all
his ears. This is a serious matter.

Palaemon. Sing on, then, since we are seated on soft
grass, and the year is at its loveliest, with growing
crops in every field, fruit coming on every tree, and
all the woods in leaf. Damoetas, you will lead off, and
Menalcas follow, replying to you every time. Alternate
song is what the Muses love.

Damoetas. Goddess of poetry, let us begin with Jove.
All the world is full of Jove. Earth owes its fruits to
him. My songs are dear to Jove.

Menalcas. And I am dear to Phoebus. He loves the
laurel and the gently blushing hyacinth. I grow them
always as a gift for him.

Damoetas. My Galatea is a saucy girl. She throws an
apple at me; then hides among the willows and hopes
that I have seen her first.

Menalcas. Ah, but my sweet Amyntas comes to me
unasked. By now he is no more a stranger to my dogs
than the Moon herself.

Damoetas. I have a present ready for my love. With
my own eyes I have marked the windy tree-top where
the doves have built.

Menalcas. I too have done my best. I have picked ten
golden apples from a tree in the woods and sent them

to my dear. I'll send another ten to-morrow.

Damoetas. To think how often Galatea talks with me! And ah the things she says! Winds, carry some of them at least to the gods' ears.

Menalcas. I know, Amyntas, in your heart of hearts you like me well. But how does that help me, if while you chase the boar I am left to mind the nets?

Damoetas. Let me have Phyllis with me for the day, Iollas, since it is my birthday. When I am offering up a heifer for the crops, then come yourself.

Menalcas. Why, Phyllis is my dearest love! She wept to see me go, and she lingered long on her 'Farewell, my beautiful Iollas!' and again 'Farewell.'

Damoetas. Wolves play the devil with the flocks; rain with the ripened corn; gales with the trees; and Amaryllis's angry moods with me.

Menalcas. Showers are delicious to the springing crops; arbutus to weaned kids; the bending willow to the mother goats. Only Amyntas pleases me.

Damoetas. Pollio loves my Muse, for all her country ways. Pierian Maidens, make a heifer the reward for one who looks so kindly on your work.

Menalcas. Pollio does more: he is busy on new poems of his own. Give him a bullock old enough to butt and kick the sand up with its heels.

Damoetas. May anyone who loves you, Pollio, attain the heights that he is happy to have seen you reach. May honey flow for him, and prickly brambles yield Assyrian spice.

Menalcas. Mevius, I hope that anyone who can put up with Bavius's verse may fall for yours. *And* let him harness foxes to the plough and milk he-goats!

Damoetas. You lads there, gathering flowers and

strawberries from their earthy beds, take to your heels!
There's a clammy snake lurking in the grass.

Menalcas. Sheep, do not venture out too far: it isn't
wise to trust this river-bank. Look at the ram himself:
his fleece is not yet dry.

Damoetas. Tityrus, head off your hungry goats from
the stream. When the time comes, I'll wash them all
myself at the spring.

Menalcas. Drive your flocks into the shade, lads. If
the sun gets at them first and dries the milk, as it did
the other day, we shall be working at their udders all
for nothing.

Damoetas. It vexes me to see how lean my bull is,
there among the fattening vetch. Love is as fatal to the
herd as to the herdsman who looks after them.

Menalcas. My flock is suffering from something even
worse: they are all skin and bones. Some evil eye must
be bewitching these young lambs of mine.

Damoetas. Read me this riddle – and I shall take you
for Apollo's self. Where in the world is the sky no
more than three yards wide?

Menalcas. Answer me this – and Phyllis shall be
yours alone. Where in the world do flowers grow with
kings' names written on them?

Palaemon. It is beyond my powers to judge between
you after such a duel. Both you, Damoetas, and
Menalcas here deserve to win a heifer. And so do all
who tremble at the approach of love's delight or know
its bitterness. Lads, drop the sluice-gates now: the
meadows have had enough to drink.

IV

THE GOLDEN AGE
RETURNS

THE GOLDEN AGE RETURNS

MUSES of Sicily, let us attempt a rather more exalted theme. Hedgerow and humble tamarisk do not appeal to all. If we must sing of woodlands, let them be such as may do a Consul honour.

We have reached the last Era in Sibylline song. Time has conceived and the great Sequence of the Ages starts afresh. Justice, the Virgin, comes back to dwell with us, and the rule of Saturn is restored. The Firstborn of the New Age is already on his way from high heaven down to earth.

With him, the Iron Race shall end and Golden Man inherit all the world. Smile on the Baby's birth, immaculate Lucina; your own Apollo is enthroned at last.

And it is in your consulship, yours, Pollio, that this glorious Age will dawn and the Procession of the great Months begin. Under your leadership all traces that remain of our iniquity will be effaced and, as they vanish, free the world from its long night of horror.

He will foregather with the gods; he will see the great men of the past consorting with them, and be himself observed by these, guiding a world to which his father's virtues have brought peace.

Free-roaming ivy, foxgloves in every dell, and smiling acanthus mingled with Egyptian lilies – these, little one, are the first modest gifts that earth, unprompted by the hoe, will lavish on you. The goats, unshepherded, will make for home with udders full of milk, and the ox will not be frightened of the lion, for all his might. Your very cradle will adorn itself with blossoms to caress you. The snake will come to grief, and poison lurk no more in the weed. Perfumes of Assyria will breathe from every hedge.

Later, when you have learnt to read the praises of the great and what your father achieved, and come to understand what manhood is, the waving corn will slowly flood the plains with gold, grapes hang in ruby clusters on the neglected thorn, and honeydew exude from the hard trunk of the oak.

Even so, faint traces of our former wickedness will linger on, to make us venture on the sea in ships, build walls around our cities, and plough the soil. With a new Tiphys at the helm, a second Argo will set out, manned by a picked heroic crew. Wars even will repeat themselves and the great Achilles be despatched to Troy once more.

Later again, when the strengthening years have made a man of you, even the trader will forsake the sea, and pine-wood ships will cease to carry merchandise for barter, each land producing all it needs. No mattock will molest the soil, no pruning-knife the vine; and then at last the sturdy ploughman will free his oxen from the yoke. Wool will be taught no more to cheat the eye with this tint or with that, but the ram himself in his own meadows will change the colour of his fleece, now to the soft glow of a purple dye, now to a saffron yellow. Lambs at their pastures will find themselves in scarlet coats.

The Fates have spoken, in concord with the unalterable decree of destiny. 'Run, spindles,' they have said. 'This is the pattern of the age to come.'

Enter – for the hour is close at hand – on your illustrious career, dear child of the gods, great increment of Jove. Look at the world, rocked by the weight of its overhanging dome; look at the lands, the far-flung seas and the unfathomable sky. See how the whole creation rejoices in the age that is to be!

Ah, if the last days of my life could only be prolonged, and breath enough remain for me to chronicle your acts, then neither Thracian Orpheus nor Linus could outsing me, not though the one had his mother and the other had his father at his side, Orpheus, his Calliope, and Linus, Apollo in all his beauty. If Pan himself, with Arcady for judge, were to contend with me, the great god Pan, with Arcady for judge, would own defeat.

Begin, then, little boy, to greet your mother with a smile: the ten long months have left her sick at heart. Begin, little boy: no one who has not given his mother a smile has ever been thought worthy of his table by a god, or by a goddess of her bed.

V

DAPHNIS AT HEAVEN'S GATE

Menalcas
Mopsus

Menalcas. Mopsus, well met. We are experts, you and I – you with the light reed-pipe, and I at song. Why not sit down together here where the hazels mingle with the elms?

Mopsus. You are my senior. It is for me to follow you, Menalcas, whether we go under the trees, where the fitful breezes make uneasy shade, or choose the shelter of the cave. Look at the mouth of it, half hidden by the scattered clusters of a woodland vine.

Menalcas. In all our hills, no one but Amyntas claims to sing as well as you.

Mopsus. Maybe; but does he not claim also to out-sing Apollo?

Menalcas. Lead off, Mopsus, with any song you know. Let it be *Phyllis and her Loves*, or *In praise of Alcon*, or *Codrus Quarrelling*. Begin: our kids are feeding; Tityrus will keep his eye on them.

Mopsus. No; there's a song I wrote out the other day on the green bark of a beech and set to music, marking the turns of voice and pipe. Let me try that one. Then you can tell Amyntas to compete!

Menalcas. If you ask me, Amyntas can stand up to you no better than the bending willow to the olive in her tender green, or meek valerian to the crimson rose. But no more talk, my lad; we are here, inside the cave.

Mopsus. When Daphis died – ah what a cruel death! – the Nymphs lamented him. The very Nymphs (you hazels and you brooks will not deny it) wept as his mother threw her arms round the poor body of her son and taxed the gods and stars with cruelty.

Nobody, Daphnis, drove the oxen from their

pastures to the cool stream in those sad days. Not one beast drank a drop, or touched a blade of grass.

The very lions of Africa gave tongue – the mountain jungle echoed their grief at Daphnis' death.

It was from Daphnis that we learnt to yoke Armenian tigers to a car, and to lead the revellers in the Bacchic dance, with vine-leaves dangling from the supple rods we wave.

As the vine beautifies the elm, and grapes the vine; as the bull ornaments the herd, and corn the happy fields; so, Daphnis, you alone shed grace on all about you.

When you were taken from us, Palēs herself withdrew, and our own Apollo left the countryside. Too often now, in furrows where we cast fat grains of barley, the wretched darnel or the unprofitable wild-oat spring up. Gone is the gentle violet, the gay narcissus gone: thistles and prickly thorns rise up instead.

Shepherds, strew leaves on the ground and screen your springs from the sun – Daphnis demands these rites. Build him a mound, and carve an epitaph on top –

> *Countrymen, Daphnis is my name:*
> *The very stars have heard my fame.*
> *Here in the woods I lived and lie –*
> *My flock was lovely: lovelier I.*

Menalcas. My heaven-born poet! Your singing is to me like sleeping on the grass when one is tired, or slaking a noon-day thirst with a fresh draught from a tumbling brook. Not only do you pipe, you sing, as sweetly as your master did. Happy young poet! His mantle falls on you.

Still, here's a song of my own I'll give you in return, as best I may, raising your Daphnis to the stars.

Yes, I will set him there among the stars; for Daphnis loved me too.

Mopsus. Could any kindness please me more? The lad himself had earned a song; and Stimichon has long been praising yours to me.

Menalcas. Clothed in new glory, Daphnis stands at Heaven's Gate, where all is wonderful, watching the clouds and stars below his feet.

It is for this that all things in the countryside, the woods themselves, Pan and the shepherds, and the Ladies of the Trees, are pierced with keen delight.

The wolves contrive no ambush for the flock; the nets are innocent of guile towards the deer. Good Daphnis stands for peace.

For very joy the shaggy mountains raise a clamour to the stars; the rocks burst into song, and the plantations speak. 'He is a god' they say; 'Menalcas, he is a god!'

Daphnis, be gracious to your friends and bring them luck. See, there are four altars here. Two of them shall be yours, two kept for sacrifices to Apollo. Here, every year, I shall offer you two cups of fresh and foaming milk and two rich bowls of olive-oil.

And best of all, we shall have merry-makings where the wine will flow, in winter by the hearth, or in the shade at harvest time. Our tankards shall be filled with the fresh nectar of the Chian grape. I will make Damoetas and Cretan Aegon sing. Alphesiboeus shall prance like any leaping Faun.

These rites are yours for ever, both when we pay our duties to the Nymphs and when we bless the fields. So long as boars prefer the mountain-heights, and fish are true to water; so long as bees eat thyme and cicadas feed on dew – your name and dignities and praises shall survive.

Just as we do to Bacchus and Ceres, we countrymen will make you yearly vows. And you, like the other gods, will see that we fulfil them.

Mopsus. What can I do, what gift can I make you, in return for such a song – sweeter, to my ear, than the music of the South Wind gathering way, or beaches beaten by the surf, or the streams that hurry down through rocky glens?

Menalcas. I will forestall you by giving you this graceful reed – the very pipe to which I owe my *Passionate Shepherd and His Love*, the same that taught me *Are These Meliboeus' Sheep?*

Mopsus. And you must take this handsome shepherd's crook, with its even knots and studs of bronze. Many's the time Antigenes begged me for it. But though he was a lad in those days whom one well might love, he never got it. Menalcas, it is yours.

VI

THE SONG OF SILENUS

To Varus

My earliest Muse, Thalia, saw fit to play with light Sicilian verse. She dwelt among the woods, and did not blush for that. Later, when kings and battles filled my thoughts, Apollo plucked my ear and gave me his advice. 'Tityrus,' he said, 'a shepherd ought to let his sheep grow fat, but court a slender Muse.'

Now, Varus, since bards enough will volunteer to sing your praises and to compose the unhappy chronicles of war, I will take up my slender reed and practise the music of the countryside. I do not sing what I have not been bidden. Yet if these lines, such as they are, should find a friend – should win one reader's heart – Varus, it will be you that all our tamarisks, every wood of ours, will celebrate. Indeed, no page could please Apollo more than one with *Varus* written at its head.

On, then, Pierian Maids!

Young Chromis and Mnasyllus came upon Silenus lying asleep in a cave, and flushed, as usual, with yesterday's wine. The garlands had slipped off his head, but they lay there close beside it, and his heavy tankard hung by its handle from the fingers that had worn it thin. They closed with him (for the old man had often raised false hopes in both of them by promising to sing), and tied him up in the very garlands he had worn. Then, as they paused in alarm, Aegle herself, the loveliest of the Naiads, came up to reinforce them and abet their deed, by staining the old man's brow and temples red with mulberry juice. He was awake by now, and smiling at their ruse. 'Shackles!' he said. 'What for? Set me free, lads. You have proved that you could catch me: that is enough. Now you shall hear the songs you wish for. They are *your* reward. Aegle, I will repay in other coin.' Then he began to sing, with no more said.

And now a miracle – you might have seen the Fauns and the wild creatures dance lightly to the tune and stubborn oak-trees wave their heads. Rocky Parnassus is not so deeply moved by the music of Apollo; Ismarus and Rhodope have never known such ecstasy when Orpheus sang.

Creation was his theme – how elements of earth, air, sea and liquid fire were massed together through the mighty void; how everything arose from these and the world itself, still soft, condensed into a globe. How next the land began to harden, to pen the Sea-god in his own domain, and slowly to assume the forms of things we know; how the first glory of the new-born Sun struck the astonished Earth; how, when the clouds were raised and rain-showers had a longer fall, the woods began to grow, and one by one beasts made their devious way through wondering hills.

Then Pyrrha throwing stones behind her to make men; the Reign of Saturn; and Prometheus tortured for his theft by eagles in the Caucasus. And Hylas – how the Argonauts had left the boy beside a spring, and shouted for him, till the long beach itself called 'Hylas', and again 'Hylas'.

So to Pasiphaë, a lady fortunate indeed if cattle had never come into the world, but lost (the pity of it!) in her passion for a snow-white bull. Ill-starred Pasiphaë, what madness seized you? Not one of Proetus' daughters, though they filled the fields with lowing like the cows they thought themselves, sank to such infamy and made a bull her mate. And yet they shrank, as cattle, from the yoke, and often felt for horns on their smooth brows. Ill-starred Pasiphaë, roaming through the hills! Meanwhile your lover rests his snow-white flank on a soft bed of hyacinths, chewing the pale grass under a dark ilex-tree, or else pursues one of the many heifers of the herd. She calls to the spirits of the Cretan woods: 'Quick, Nymphs, and close the forest glades while there is hope that I may light upon one imprint of that roving hoof. Maybe a bank of green grass took his fancy, or he may have kept up with the herd, and in the end be brought home by some heifers to the stalls at Gortyn.'

And then the maiden who coveted, too much, an apple from the Gardens of the West; and the sisters of Phaethon, incased in moss and bitter bark, planted as alders, and made to shoot up from the ground.

Another scene – how Gallus wandering by the waters of Permessus met a Muse, one of the Nine, who led him into the Aonian Hills, where the whole choir of Phoebus rose as one in honour of the mortal man, and Linus, godlike singer of the countryside, whose head was garlanded with flowers and bitter parsley leaves, said to him: 'This reed-pipe – take it from my hand – the Muses give to you; the very pipe they gave the Bard of Ascra long ago, which he played when he sang the stubborn ash-trees down the mountain-side. Sing to this pipe the tale of the Grynean Wood, till not a grove is left in which Apollo takes a greater pride.'

And must we follow him as he went on to sing of Scylla, Nisus' child, whom story pictures as a lovely woman with a ring of howling monsters round her waist, harrying Odysseus' ships, and with her sea-dogs' fangs tearing the flesh (ah horror!) of his trembling men, down in the whirlpool's depths? Or as he sang of Tereus' altered shape, of the dish that Philomela cooked for him, and the gift that followed it, of her swift flight into the wilderness, and of the unpractised wings on which the hapless Queen had hovered first above the roof-top that had once been hers?

Indeed, he gave them all the songs that once upon a time Eurotas, happy river, heard from Phoebus' lips and bade his laurels get by heart. All these Silenus sang. The music struck the valleys and the valleys tossed it to the stars – till the lads were warned to drive home and to count their sheep, by Vesper, as he trod unwelcome into the listening sky.

VII

THE SINGING-MATCH

Meliboeus
Corydon
Thyrsis

Meliboeus. As luck would have it, Daphnis had just sat down under a whispering ilex-tree, when Corydon and Thyrsis each drove up his flock to the same place, Thyrsis his sheep, and Corydon his she-goats with their udders full of milk – a pair of graceful lads, Arcadians both, and each as ready as the other to lead off with a song, or to give an apt response.

And now my own he-goat, the father of my flock, who had slipped off as I was fencing young myrtles from the cold, went wandering up to them. Thus, I caught sight of Daphnis. He saw me too, and called across to me: 'Quick, Meliboeus, join us here. Your goat is safe; so are the kids. Rest in the shade, if you have time to spare. As for your bullocks, when they want a drink, they will find their own way through the meadows to this very spot, where the Mincius embroiders his banks with a green fringe of bending rushes, and the sacred oak is loud with swarming bees.'

What ought I to have done? I had no Phyllis or Alcippe to pen my new-weaned lambs at home. Yet Corydon and Thyrsis were bound to make a famous match of it. I put my business in the second place, and their amusements first.

So the pair set to, singing alternately against each other. Their Muse insisted on this plan. Corydon sang his lines, and Thyrsis followed him in each case with an answering set.

Corydon. Nymphs of Libethrum, dearly loved by me, either let me sing as you let Codrus sing, Codrus my friend, a poet second only to Apollo; or, if we cannot all attain such heights, I shall hang up my tuneful flute, here on this pine, and make the tree your own.

Thyrsis. Bring ivy-leaves to decorate your rising poet, shepherds of Arcady, and so make Codrus burst his sides with envy. Or, if he tries to harm me with excessive praise, twine foxglove round my brows, to stop his evil tongue from hurting your predestined bard.

Corydon. Delian Maid, young Micon dedicates this bristly boar's head and the branching antlers of a long-lived stag to you. And if this luck holds good, you shall stand here, carved in smooth marble, whole, with scarlet hunting-boots laced round your legs.

Thyrsis. This bowl of milk and these honey-cakes, Priapus, are all you can hope for in the year, guarding a poor man's garden as you do. You are made of marble now – we can afford no more. But listen. If the flock multiplies at lambing-time, you shall be gold.

Corydon. My Galatea, Lady of the Sea, sweeter to me than Hyblaean thyme, more lovely than pale ivy, brighter than any swan, come to me early, come when the bulls begin to leave their pastures for the byre, if your love, Corydon, is in your thoughts at all.

Thyrsis. Indeed now, you may think of me as bitterer than Sardinian herbs, rougher than butcher's-broom, cheaper than sea-weed cast up on the beach, if this day has not been already longer than a year. Home with you, bullocks: you have had enough. Is there no shame in you? Home with you now!

Corydon. You mossy springs, and banks of grass softer than sleep; you green arbutuses that cast the net-work of your shade across them; comfort our sheep under midsummer suns. The burning days are coming in and the buds already swelling on the tender shoots of the vine.

Thyrsis. Here is the hearth, logs rich in resin, a big fire all the time, and doorposts blackened by the constant smoke. We care as little here about the North Wind and the cold as a wolf cares for numbers, or rivers for their banks in time of spate.

Corydon. Here prickly chestnuts stand, and junipers. Everywhere the fruit lies strewn under its parent tree. The whole world smiles. But if the handsome Alexis were to leave our hills, you might see even the rivers running dry.

Thyrsis. The fields are parched, and the grass is dying of thirst – it is this wicked weather! The Wine-god has begrudged the hillsides even the shadow that the vine-leaves gave. But when our Phyllis comes, the woods will all rejoice in green, and happy showers will fall in plenty from the sky.

Corydon. Hercules loves poplars best of all; Bacchus prefers the vine; Venus, the Queen of Beauty, loves the myrtle best; and Apollo his own bays. Phyllis is fond of hazels. As long as Phyllis likes them best, neither the myrtle nor Apollo's bays shall take a higher place than hazels.

Thyrsis. The ash in forests is the loveliest tree; the pine in gardens; the poplar by the river's bank; and the fir-tree on the mountain-heights. But if you, my handsome Lycidas, will spend more time with me, the ash in her own forest and the pine-tree in the garden must give place to you.

Meliboeus. So much I can recall. Thyrsis put up a fight, but all in vain. He lost; and from that day it has been Corydon, Corydon every time with us.

VIII

DAMON AND ALPHESIBOEUS

DAMON AND ALPHESIBOEUS

DAMON and Alphesiboeus, singing in rivalry – let us record their pastoral melodies. A heifer heard their songs with such delight that she forgot to crop the grass; the very lynxes were bemused; and brooks, arrested, paused in their downward course. Damon and Alphesiboeus – let us commemorate the shepherds' Muse.

But where are you for whom I sing? Skirting, by now, the mighty barrier of Timavus' rocks? Coasting the shores of the Illyrian Sea? ... Ah, will the day ever come when I shall be allowed to chronicle your deeds? Will the day come when I can celebrate your tragedies, sole rivals of the Muse of Sophocles, through all the world? My first notes were inspired by you: for you my last will sound. Accept this poem, begun at your command, and let its ivy twine with the victor's laurels round your brow.

It was the hour when the cold shade of Night has scarcely faded from the sky, the time when dew on tender grass is most delicious to the sheep, that Damon chose to start his song, leaning against the smooth trunk of an olive-tree.

Damon. O Morning Star be born, and bring in friendly day, while I, duped by my love for my unfaithful Nysa, make this lament and force the gods, though the vows they heard from us have brought me little good, to listen yet to the last utterance of one who will soon be dead.

Reed-pipe of Maenalus, support me in my song.

On Maenalus the woods make music always and the

pine-trees speak. His hills for ever listen to the loves of shepherd lads, and Pan himself, the first that could not brook the silence of the reeds.

Reed-pipe of Maenalus, support me in my song.

So Nysa marries Mopsus! What may we lovers not expect? Griffins will mate with mares, and, in the years to be, the timid doe will come and drink from the same basin as the hounds. Cut yourself wedding-torches, Mopsus, for the bride is yours. Fling nuts in the air, as bridegrooms do. It is for you the Evening Star deserts his mountain bed.

Reed-pipe of Maenalus, support me in my song.

A worthy husband and a worthy bride! – Nysa, who spurns the crowd; who loathes my flute, my goats, my shaggy eyebrows and my straggling beard; who thinks there are no gods to keep an eye on what a woman does.

Reed-pipe of Maenalus, support me in my song.

You were a child, Nysa, when I saw you first, you and your mother, gathering apples wet with dew. It was in our garden, and I acted as your guide. I was just tall enough to reach the laden branches from the ground, though not yet twelve myself. At the first look, I perished; at the first look, my soul was lost to me.

Reed-pipe of Maenalus, support me in my song.

At last I know what Love is really like. That Boy was never made of flesh and blood like us. His cradle is the native rock, of Tmaros or of Rhodope, or the remote Saharan wilderness.

Reed-pipe of Maenalus, support me in my song.

Love has no pity in him. He taught a mother, once, to stain her hands with her own children's blood. A cruel mother – yes; but was she worse than that remorseless Boy? A cruel heart indeed – but oh, the malice of the Boy!

Reed-pipe of Maenalus, support me in my song.

Now let the wolf, with none to drive him, fly in panic from the lamb. Let the hard oak bring golden apples forth; narcissus bloom on alders; drops of rich amber sweat from tamarisk bark. Let the screech-owl outsing the swan; let Tityrus become an Orpheus, an Orpheus in the woods, or an Arion with the dolphins round him.

Reed-pipe of Maenalus, support me in my song.

No, let the deep sea overwhelm the world. Woodlands, good-bye to you; I will go up to the windy lookout on the mountain-top and plunge down headlong to the waves. Let Nysa take this last gift from a dying man.

Reed-pipe of Maenalus, be still: my song is done.

So Damon sang. What Alphesiboeus sang in answer, it is for you to say, Pierian goddesses. We cannot all succeed in every task.

Alphesiboeus. Bring water out and wreathe this altar with soft strands of wool. Burn rich vervain and manly frankincense, that I may see what sorcery will do to stir that unimpassioned man of mine. Nothing is wanting here but magic spells.

Bring Daphnis from the town, my spells, bring Daphnis home.

Spells can pull down the Moon herself from heaven. Circe with spells transformed Odysseus' men. Sing the right spell and you can blast the clammy snakes that live in the fields.

Bring Daphnis from the town, my spells, bring Daphnis home.

I take three threads – three colours pick them out – and bind them round you first. Next, I walk round this altar with your effigy, three times. Odd numbers please the gods.

Bring Daphnis from the town, my spells, bring Daphnis home.

Twine the three colours, Amaryllis, in three knots. Come, twine them, Amaryllis, and say: 'These are the chains of Venus that I twine.'

Bring Daphnis from the town, my spells, bring Daphnis home.

This clay is hardened, and this wax is melted, by the selfsame fire. So may the fire of my love act on Daphnis. Scatter the salted grain and kindle crackling twigs of bay with pitch. The heartless Daphnis burns me up: I burn these bays to deal with *him.*

Bring Daphnis from the town, my spells, bring Daphnis home.

May Daphnis be possessed by such a yearning as a heifer feels when, worn out by a long search for her mate through copses and tall forest trees, she sinks down on the green sedge by a running water, forlorn, forgetting even to go home as the dusk deepens into night. May Daphnis know desire like that, and I not care to cure it.

Bring Daphnis from the town, my spells, bring Daphnis home.

Long since, the unfaithful wretch left in my hands these things that he had worn, my sweet securities for him. These pledges, Mother-Earth, I put into your charge, here at my very gate. Daphnis is owing to me on the strength of these.

Bring Daphnis from the town, my spells, bring Daphnis home.

Moeris himself gave me these herbs and magic simples gathered in the land of Pontus. They grow in plenty there. Many's the time I have seen Moeris, with their help, change into a wolf and vanish in the woods. I have seen him call up ghosts from deep down in the grave, and shift a standing crop from one field to another.

Bring Daphnis from the town, my spells, bring Daphnis home.

Up with the ashes, Amaryllis! Take them out, and throw them over your shoulder into the running water. But do not turn your head to look. It is through them that I shall get at Daphnis – not that he cares a jot about the gods or magic spells.

Bring Daphnis from the town, my spells, bring Daphnis home.

Look, the whole altar is alight with flickering flame! The ashes I was going to move have come to life without my touching them. Ah, may this mean good luck! Something will surely come of it. And there is Hylax, barking at the gate. Can it be true? Or is it nothing but a lover's fancy and an idle dream?

Be still, my spells: he is coming from the town. Be still now: he is here.

IX

THE ROAD TO TOWN

Lycidas
Moeris

Lycidas. Moeris, where are you off to? This is the road to town. Is that where you are bound?

Moeris. Oh, Lycidas, a blow has fallen on us – one we never even feared. That I should live to see a total stranger seize our farm and say, 'This is my property: be off!' – to us who have always worked the land! Now, we are a miserable, beaten crew; and, as would happen in this topsy-turvy world, it is for him that I'm taking in these kids – bad luck go with them!

Lycidas. But surely I had heard that all the land was saved, from where the hills fall back and leave a ridge to drop down with an easy slope, to the water and the old beeches with the battered tops – saved by your dear Menalcas and his poetry?

Moeris. No doubt you had. A rumour did go round. But this poetry of ours, Lycidas, can do no more against a man in arms than the doves we have heard of at Dodona, when an eagle comes their way. In fact, if a timely raven on my left hand in the hollow ilex had not warned me at all costs to cut short this last dispute, neither your friend Moeris nor Menalcas himself would be alive to-day.

Lycidas. Could anyone conceive such wickedness? To think, Menalcas, how near we came to losing you and, with you, all you did to cheer our lives! Who would have sung to us about the Nymphs? Who would have strewn wild flowers on the ground or given our springs green cover from the sun? Who else could have written the lines I overheard you sing the other day, quite unaware of me, as you were on your way to see our darling Amaryllis? –

Feed my goats, Tityrus, while I am gone – I shan't be long.

*And take them to the stream when they have fed. But watch
the he-goat, Tityrus, as you go, and give him a wide berth.
He is apt to butt.*

Moeris. Still better, though it isn't polished yet, the
poem to Varus that he was working on –

*Varus, if only Mantua is spared to us – poor Mantua, too
near for happiness to doomed Cremona – your name shall be
extolled to heaven by our singing swans.*

Lycidas. Do lead off now, with anything of his you
know – and may your bees swarm on no Corsican
yews; may your cows feed on clover till their udders
cannot hold the milk. I too am a poet who has found
some favour with the Muse. I too have written songs.
I too have heard the shepherds call me bard. But I take
it from them with a grain of salt: I have the feeling that
I cannot yet compare with Varius or Cinna, but cackle
like a goose among melodious swans.

Moeris. I am trying to please you, Lycidas. While
you were speaking, I have been cudgelling my brains
in the attempt to recollect a song I knew – and not a
bad one either –

*Come here, my Galatea. What is there to amuse you in the
sea? Spring, the gay spring, is here. Here by the stream all
kinds of flowers are blooming on the turf. Here a bright
poplar sways above my cave, and the dangling vines weave
shadows on the ground. Come here, and let the wild waves
hammer on the beach.*

Lycidas. What of the one I heard you sing to yourself
under a starry sky? I know the tune – if only I could
recollect the words –

*Daphnis, why study the ascent of constellations that have
had their day? See how Olympian Caesar's star has climbed
into the sky – the star to gladden all our corn with grain and*

paint the grapes with purple on the sun-bathed hills. Graft your pears, Daphnis, now; your children's children will enjoy the fruit.

Moeris. Time carries everything away, even our memories. How often as a boy I sang through the long summer day and put the sun to bed! So many songs forgotten! And now my very voice is failing me. The wolves saw Moeris first. Well, never mind; Menalcas will recite these poems to you to your heart's content.

Lycidas. All this procrastination whets my appetite. Now is the moment – look around! Through all its length the lake lies calm and hushed for you; the blustering wind has fallen: not a murmur left. Here too we are just half-way: Bianor's tomb is coming into sight. Here where the countrymen are thinning out the leaves, here, Moeris, let us sing. Rest your kids now, and we shall still reach town. Or, if it looks as though the night might turn to rain before we are in, why not go forward singing all the way? It makes the going easier. I will relieve you of that load; then we could walk and sing at the same time.

Moeris. No more, my lad. Let us stick to the business in hand. As for Menalcas' songs, we shall sing them all the better when he comes to us himself.

X

GALLUS

GALLUS

Yet one more task, with your help, Arethusa, and I have done – a little poem to my beloved Gallus (who could refuse him that?), and for Lycoris too to read.

Begin, and may your stream slide under the Sicilian waves unmingled with the harsh sea-brine. Begin, and let us tell the tale of Gallus' troubled love, while the snub-nosed she-goats crop the tender shoots. We are not singing to the deaf: the forest echoes every word.

Where were you, gentle Naiads, in what high woods or in what glades, while Gallus lay dying of unrequited love? Nothing detained you on Parnassus; nothing on any ridge of Pindus; and nothing at Aonian Aganippe's spring. Yet even the laurels, even the tamarisks, wept for Gallus; for Gallus, lying by his lonely rock, even pine-clad Maenalus and the cold cliffs of Lycaeus wept.

The very sheep have gathered round. They think no ill of us: think none of them, my heaven-born poet. Even the lovely Adonis grazed flocks along a stream.

The shepherd came; and the lumbering swineherds followed. Menalcas too, wet from gathering acorns in autumnal woods. All of them asked you: 'How did you come to lose your heart?'

Apollo came. 'Gallus,' he said, 'what madness is this? Lycoris, your darling, has run off with another man, over the snows, to share the rigours of a soldier's life.'

Even Silvanus came, in all his woodland pride, with flowering fennel and tall lilies nodding from his head.

Pan came, the god of Arcady, as I myself have seen him, stained with vermilion and with blood-red elder-berry juice. 'Enough, enough!' he cried. 'Love is not moved by such distress. You will no more satisfy the cruel god with tears than goats with leaves, or bees with clover, or the grass by watering it.'

But Gallus, still disconsolate, said: 'Come what may, you, my Arcadian friends, will sing of all this to your hills – and what songs are there like the songs of Arcady? How peacefully my bones would lie, lulled by your reed-pipes making music of my love!

'Indeed I wish I had been one of you, a shepherd of your flocks, or a vineyard hand. Phyllis might then have been my sweetheart, or Amyntas, or some other love. And is Amyntas dark? Well, what of that? Violets are dark, and so are blueberries. We should have lain together, among the willows, under the bending vines. Phyllis would have picked me garlands, and Amyntas sung for me.

'Here, my Lycōris, you would find cool springs, soft meadows, woods. Here, with you by me, I could endure the wastage of the years.

'But as it is, insensate loyalty to the stern god of War keeps me in arms where weapons fly and the enemy make their stand; while you (must I believe such cruelty?) have left your country to set eyes, alone, without me, on the Alpine snows and frozen Rhine. Ah, may the frost not hurt you; may the sharp ice not cut your dainty feet!

'I will go now and tune to the Sicilian shepherd's pipe the poems I once wrote in Chalcidic verse. I am resolved: I choose the hard life in the forest, where the wild beasts have their caves. I'll carve my love on sapling trees: as the trees grow, so will my love. And I meanwhile will wander with the Nymphs on Maenalus, or hunt the savage boar. No frost shall hinder me from drawing coverts on Parthenius with my hounds. I see

myself already, climbing the crags; I hear the echoes
as I thread the woods; a Cretan arrow flies from my
Parthian bow – and I am happy.

'As though such things could be a cure for my
disease! As though the god of Love could soften to the
sufferings of men! No; all is over. Tree-nymphs and
poetry itself have ceased to please. Even you have
failed, woodlands; away with you! Nothing I might
endure could change a god like him – not if I were to
face the sleet and snow of Macedonian skies and drink
from the Hebrus in midwinter weather; not if I chose,
when the dry bark hangs dying on the elms, to shepherd Ethiopian sheep under the tropic sun. Love
carries all before him: I too must yield to Love.'

Pierian goddesses, let these lines suffice for your poet
to have sung, as he sat and wove a basket with slim
marsh-mallow twigs. I count on you to make the most
of them to Gallus – Gallus, my love for whom grows
as much hour by hour as the green alder shoots up
when the spring is young.

Now let us go. The shade is bad for singers. This is
a juniper: its shade is bad. Even crops suffer in the
shade.

Home with you, goats: you have had your fill.
Hesper is coming: home with you, goats.

ESSAYS ON THE
ECLOGUES

THE DISPOSSESSED

'I sang of you, Tityrus, under the awning of a spreading beech.'   *Georgics*, IV, 566.

IN the first words of the First Eclogue, Virgil sounds the keynote of the whole work. With Tityrus practising woodland melodies on his pipe, he invites us into the Arcady that he has seen. But a conflicting note follows fast on the first theme. With 'Exile for me, Tityrus', we are once more in touch with the world of fact – a world less real than the other, if reality can be held to admit of degrees, yet persistently intrusive none the less. The conflict between these two themes makes a beautiful poem of what might only have been a pretty one.

It means also that to appreciate the poem we should know something of its setting and understand the circumstances in which Meliboeus has just been ousted from his farm, while the more fortunate Tityrus is left in possession of his meagre holding by the authorities in Rome. Nor have the critics ever stopped asking whether Virgil imagined this little drama in a spirit of altruistic sympathy with the Italian countryman's passionate attachment to the soil, or whether he wishes us to understand that he is recording experiences of his own. In other words, is Virgil either 'Tityrus' or 'Meliboeus' in this Eclogue, and 'Menalcas' in the Ninth, or is he no more than the creator of all three characters?

The evictions were real enough. They occurred all too frequently during the period of civil war that followed the assassination of Julius Caesar in 44 B.C.

Virgil's native province in Northern Italy suffered heavily at the hands of the Commissioners appointed by Octavian (the future Emperor Augustus) to find lands for the settlement of his discharged veterans; and the territories of Cremona, with some of the farmlands of its neighbour Mantua, were seized for this purpose after his victory over Brutus and Cassius at Philippi in 42 B.C.

But that, I think, is all we need to know of contemporary events in order to enjoy the poem, and all that Virgil himself intended us to bear in mind when reading it. I do not believe that he wished us to take either Tityrus or Meliboeus for himself. He is their creator. If he is either, he is both of them – Tityrus singing for ever under his spreading beech and Meliboeus never ceasing to lament for his once prosperous flock.

Yet, since most of the scholars have not been content to leave it at that, we should perhaps examine a little more closely the personal and historical problems which a different reading of the Eclogue raises, admitting that we should be glad to glean from it any facts of Virgil's external life that can be legitimately inferred.

First then, is there anything to prove that Virgil or his family did lose their Mantuan farm in the course of these high-handed proceedings? The only contemporary evidence outside the *Eclogues* is a little poem[1] by the youthful Virgil himself, clearly written at a distance from home (possibly at Naples) and suggesting that some calamity was threatening his father in their home province. We have to wait a long time before this very

1. *Villula quae Sironis eras*, etc. I should add that it is by no means universally accepted as genuine.

meagre clue is supplemented. The later evidence is
gleaned from a life of Virgil compiled by Probus,
possibly in Nero's reign; an epigram by Martial, who
wrote under Domitian; another *Life*, known as that of
Donatus, which probably originated with Suetonius
in the time of Hadrian; and finally from the much later
commentators known as Donatus and Servius. Probus
tells one story, Martial another, and Suetonius combines and confuses the two. The later biographers, who
drew on Suetonius, only add further complexity and
uncertainty to the tale – not unnaturally, since, in my
opinion, they and their predecessors all went for their
details to the poems themselves, and these, however
closely questioned, give us anything but a straightforward and unified account. We shall never know the
facts. And, even if we did know that the farm was
seized, we might still be wrong in thinking that Virgil,
in this Eclogue and the Ninth, is recording his own
experiences, rather than giving an impersonal but
sympathetic picture of the husbandmen's difficulties in
troubled times.

However, the tale, for what it is worth, runs roughly
as follows. Virgil is Tityrus in the First Eclogue and
Menalcas in the Ninth. After an unsuccessful petition
presented to the authorities in poetical form, he is
deprived of his ancestral lands by one or other of three
Commissioners, Pollio, Varus, and Gallus; travels to
Rome in search of restitution; and obtains it from
Octavian, who causes one of the three to rescind the
eviction order made by his colleague or predecessor.
Further, on returning north to resume possession, he is
attacked by the new occupant (a centurion named
Arrius in some accounts), and saves his life only by

plunging into the River Mincius and swimming to the
farther bank.[1]

As I have already suggested, this circumstantial
though varied account can, if one is in the right mood
for the task, be built up readily from the poems themselves, even to the last picturesque detail, which is
founded on the incident in the Third Eclogue where
the ram gets a wetting in the stream. But I must warn
the reader that if he takes this allegorical view of the
Eclogues, he will not have an easy case to handle.
Indeed it is beset with assumptions and difficulties.

For instance, it is only guesswork to identify with
Mantua the market town that the shepherds refer to as
their own. They do not name it. It is also an assumption, though perhaps a more likely one, that the 'god'
who gives Tityrus his blessing in Rome is to be taken
for Octavian. Then there is the question of Virgil's
pseudonyms. On a special occasion, in the Sixth
Eclogue, he does for once call himself Tityrus; so there
is some reason for thinking that the young poet may
be the greybeard Tityrus in the First. But, if so, he
saves his farm; whereas, if we allow him by some
caprice to have become Menalcas in the Ninth, the
farm is lost. So why not make him Meliboeus here? If
we do that, we shall at any rate have lost his farm for
him, as we set out to do. And three different disguises
in a single book are scarcely worse than two. The
alternative is to suppose that in the course of a few
pages he congratulates himself on the restitution of his
farm and condoles with himself on its loss – which
would at least be odd, though perhaps not impossible.

But real absurdity is achieved when the critics, for-

1. See also p. 96.

getting that the allegory is an assumption of their own, round on the innocent Virgil for describing *himself* as going to Rome in two inconsistent capacities, as a land-owner, to recover his farm, and as a serf, to purchase his freedom.

My net feeling is that Virgil is not reporting his own or his father's misfortunes. He is certainly referring to contemporary events, and he may be transmuting his experience of life, as poets will; for even the most imaginative writer must at some point make his contacts with external reality. But further than this I, for one, feel that we must not go.

After digressing on these problems at perhaps too great a length, I will add nothing to what I have already said about the beauty of this moving poem, lest I explain it all away. I will even leave the reader to discover Tennyson's indebtedness to Virgil by himself. But a word on the topography of the *Eclogues* will not come amiss at this point.

Their scenery was for a long time held to be composite. Here, for instance, the beech trees, the mountains and the high rocks suggest the Sicilian landscape, while on the other hand the marshy surroundings of the little farm are more typical of the valley of the River Po in Northern Italy. But R. S. Conway made out a strong case for the poet's accuracy in his Harvard Lecture, *Where Was Virgil's Farm?* and convinced some scholars that he is faithfully describing the country round his own birthplace, in a village near the foothills of the Alps and at a greater distance from the low-lying town of Mantua than had hitherto been supposed. On the other hand, Tenney Frank, in his *Vergil: A Biography*, maintains that the poet wrote at Naples and that the scenery of his pastoral poems is for the most part Neapolitan. The latest contribution to the problem comes from H. J. Rose, who, in his recent book, *The Eclogues of Vergil*, suggests that the poet is in the main relying on memories of summer holidays spent with the shepherds in their *highland* pastures in the lower Alps. This, in my opinion, comes nearer to the truth. Virgil, as poets often do, wrote from his memory and his imagination. His scenes have a natural consistency, but he is no more to be cross-examined on topographical details than is Housman in his *Shropshire Lad*.

Whatever they may make of these divergent views of the scenery of the *Eclogues*, British readers will be amused to see their own country referred to in terms that they themselves might use of Tierra del Fuego. When Virgil wrote, Britain had not yet been brought within the confines of the Roman Empire. Julius Caesar had made a landing there in 55 B.C., and a reconnaissance in force in 54, but on each occasion our forefathers had acquitted themselves against him with their usual obstinacy; and it was not till much later, under the Emperor Claudius, that the island, or rather its southern part, was overrun and occupied by the Roman legions.

II

THE PASSIONATE SHEPHERD
TO HIS LOVE

In the Second Eclogue, Virgil has set himself the difficult task of creating a unified poem out of what he himself describes as 'shreds of song'. And these must be 'disordered' – or he departs from his own programme. The skill by which each disjointed utterance is made to lead into the next, each intervening thought is left unspoken yet revealed, so that the completed chain emerges as an integral whole, is consummate.

The Eclogue is exceptional too in another respect. Elsewhere for the most part, when the sun begins to overpower us, we are led under the shadow of the leafy trees or into the still cooler recesses of a mossy cavern. But here, with Corydon in his lovelorn rambles, we are exposed to the blistering heat of the summer sun, while the high, insistent drumming of the cicada dins our ears.

But most of the critics, at any rate up to the end of the 19th century, seem concerned not so much with Virgil's poetical achievement as with the ethical questions raised by his choice of a subject. Servius, writing long before our own Shakespeare addressed sonnets to a youth, and imbued with the idea that a poet is generally to be identified with one of the characters whose feelings he describes, makes no bones of the matter at all. According to him, Corydon is Virgil, and Virgil loved a youth called Alexander (disguised here as Alexis), whom his friend Pollio gave him at a dinner-party after Virgil had complimented him on the lad's good looks. Servius has the grace to add that there was nothing reprehensible about this affection.

Conington, in commenting on this Eclogue in connection with Servius's gossip, makes a remark which I quote as typical of Victorian criticism at its most pompous and obtuse. 'We should be glad,' he says, 'to believe it to be purely imaginary, though even then it is sufficiently degrading to Virgil.'[1] On the other hand, Sellar, in his book on the poet, will have none of this nonsense. He appeals on behalf of Virgil's morals to the unanimous opinion of his friends and to the impression of integrity and purity which his work makes on our minds. Wordsworth's appreciation too is reassuring.[2] And so is Macaulay's. The latter not only preferrred the *Eclogues* to the *Georgics* and the *Aeneid*, but of the Eclogues liked the Tenth and the Second best. We can surely accept without qualms what Lord Macaulay blessed, and leave Virgil's reputation in these able hands.

However, it will not be out of place to add a word or two here on what the Greeks and Romans have to say about the passion of love. To them, if we may take their more thoughtful writers as representing the best public opinion, love was a divine phenomenon, whatever form it took, an ecstasy to be studied dispassionately, though not without awe, as the visitation of a powerful influence external to man. They expressed

1. John Conington, *The Works of Virgil*, Vol. I (1858).
2. W. Y. Sellar (*Virgil*, p. 172) quotes from S. Coleridge's *Memoirs*, Vol. II, p. 411 as follows: 'I am much pleased to see (writes S. Coleridge) how highly Mr Wordsworth speaks of Virgil's style, and of his Bucolics, which I have ever thought most graceful and tender. They are quite another thing from Theocritus, however they may be based on Theocritus.'

this feeling by making the goddess Aphrodite and her son Eros (the Roman Venus and her son Cupid) responsible between them for all that happens in the poor lover's heart. Homer, in Book XXIII of the *Odyssey*, causes Penelope, the constant queen, to excuse or at least condone the infidelity of the notorious Helen by attributing her infatuation to the temptation of the goddess. Sophocles's most memorable epithet of Eros is 'unconquerable in battle'. Virgil himself, when dealing, in the Sixth Eclogue, with a far more abnormal attachment than that of Corydon, the legendary Pasiphaë's passion for a bull, hastens to commiserate the ill-starred lady before he contrasts her infamy with the integrity of Proetus' daughters. And again, in the Eighth, we hear how Cupid 'taught' Medea, still in love with the faithless Jason, to murder the children she had borne him; and Virgil leaves us in doubt which of the two, Medea or the god, he thinks is most to blame.

But no Greek or Roman writer presents the whole picture so clearly as does Plato in his *Symposium*. Here love is studied in its upward progress from the lowest to the highest threshold, and looking through the philosopher's eyes we learn to appreciate the Greek idea that in all love, however mundane, provided it be absolute and self-obliterating, there lurks a divine spark which shows its kinship with the consuming fire that is the love of God.

III

ARE THESE MELIBOEUS' SHEEP?

'Alternate song delights the Muse.'
Eclogue III, 59

SERVIUS, though he seems not to rank the rather acrimonious Third Eclogue as high as some of the others, is yet careful to point out that variety is the essence of pastoral poetry and that Virgil was justified in enriching his collection by adding to it this picture of his shepherd songsters in less genial mood. I think we may be even more grateful to Virgil than Servius suggests. The whole poem goes with a swing. Not only is the preliminary backchat of the shepherds both fast and entertaining, but when they at last settle down to their duel, we enjoy a delightful combat of wits, with a subtlety and speed of thrust and parry that challenge the closest attention. Moreover, in this and the Seventh Eclogues, we feel that Virgil comes nearer than in any other part of his book to the type of extemporary contest with which we can suppose the real shepherds of the ancient world to have amused themselves during the long days they spent among Arcadian or Sicilian hills.

In such contests, for which the technical term is amoebaean, one of the singers leads off with a short song of a few lines on a theme of his own choice, and is immediately followed by his rival with an utterance of equal length on the same or a contrasted theme, designed to cap, refute, or in some way improve upon the lines it answers. The first singer then proceeds either to open another aspect of the theme, or to broach a new topic, which his opponent must deal with as before. One would have thought that the challenger would be handicapped by being allotted the second place, which must surely have taxed the invention and wit of the contestants far more than the first. But this was not so. Here, for instance, Damoetas, the challenger, though he offers to waive his right to the first place, is ordered by the umpire to begin.

Amoebaean singing must indeed have been a difficult and a fascinating art. To-day it is still true that 'alternate song delights the Muse': we have it yet in several forms. But alternate *improvization* is another matter, and I know of no school of modern singers or crooners whose efforts in that direction I am anxious to hear. On the other hand I am told by members of our forces who have been in Cyprus that the art is still practised and held in high esteem in that island.

The little songs themselves were of course for the most part dramatic in form. I mean that the singer, like any modern entertainer, sang, as often as not, in an assumed rôle, as when Menalcas answers Damoetas's request to Iollas for the loan of Phyllis with an indignant reply in the name of Iollas himself. The settings too are imaginary. Damoetas's sudden discovery of a snake in the grass is *not* a signal for his audience to disperse.

Unfortunately, these facts, so obvious that I hesitated to mention them, have afforded encouragement once more to the commentators who find hidden meanings in all these poems of Virgil. For instance, Servius, not content to let Menalcas recall an occasion when the ram of his flock has ventured too near the river-bank and fallen in, tells us that the shepherd is speaking for

Virgil and referring to the alleged fact that the poet escaped from the centurion who had seized his farm only by plunging into the River Mincius. At the same time it must be said on Servius's behalf that he can administer a neat rebuke when he detects his own foible in others. To those who would have us read into Menalcas's gift of ten apples to his love Virgil's dedication of his ten Eclogues to Augustus, he tartly replies: 'A superfluous suggestion. Why drag in allegory here?' And he scores too when he points out how Palaemon stems the flow of song from the two lads by the timely 'allegory' of his concluding words.

However there certainly are some places in the poem where we must allow that Virgil has caused his shepherds to express his own opinions; for instance where he compliments his friend and patron Pollio as a critic and a poet; and where he rounds on Mevius and Bavius, two contemporary writers of whom we know little more than that they had ventured to disparage his work.

Finally, there are the two riddles with which the contest comes to an end. Here, at the risk of disappointing crossword addicts, I am going to fall back on the naive comment that Servius makes (after cataloguing a number of peculiarly unsatisfactory answers). 'It must,' he says, 'be admitted that, like most others, these enigmas do not lend themselves to any obvious solution.' He also tells us that Virgil was reported to have said, with reference to the first of them, that he had 'set a trap for the scholars'. If that is so, I hope to be excused if I give it a wide berth.

IV

THE GOLDEN AGE RETURNS

'What could I not have made of you, if I had found you
still alive?'

> *Words put into the mouth of St Paul, standing before*
> *Virgil's tomb at Naples, by an unknown Christian poet.*

No short poem in any language has been so much discussed as the Fourth Eclogue. In a brief essay one can
do little more than suggest the fascination and the
complexity of the controversies it has aroused.

Our best approach to them will be to review, in a
simplified form, the three main interpretations that can
be put upon the poem – the lyrical, the political, and
the Messianic.

I

First, then, it is not impossible to accept the Eclogue
simply as a lyrical utterance, a poet's expression of
delight at the prospect of returning peace, an ebullition
on which no deep or definite meaning should be forced.
Reading it in this mood, we should have to underline
the word 'rather' in the first sentence; to ask how
Virgil, if he attached momentous significance to the
poem, came to include it in a volume he repeatedly
refers to as a collection of light verse; to stress the fact
that we are still in the woodlands, still surrounded by
the goats and sheep of the rural scene; and to assume
that, when these friendly and familiar beasts surprise
us by their apocalyptic behaviour, Virgil is only
indulging in one of those playful moments that are so

characteristic of his pastoral Muse. At the same time
we shall have great difficulty in discounting the strictly
factual, if not precise, prophecies and the very concrete
conception of a Wonder-child that he has seen fit to
introduce into the work. If, as I do, the reader finds it
impossible to dismiss these as the mere by-product of
a lyrical impulse, we had better pass on to the next
interpretation and see how the poem reads as a straightforward political prophecy.

II

Here everything runs smoothly – up to a point. If
we begin by asking from what source Virgil derived
the peculiar form in which his oracle is cast, we have
not far to seek. The idea of cyclical World-Ages was
familiar to Graeco-Roman thought, and the doctrine
of eternal recurrence,[1] which he enunciates when he
says that Achilles must return to Troy, is found in
Greek philosophy from the time of Pythagoras[2] to
that of the Stoics and beyond. All this was part of
Virgil's education. Nor is it difficult to guess where he
went for the central idea of a Wonder-child on which
he hangs his general theme. When, in the first lines of
the poem, he refers us to 'Sibylline song', he has
admitted his source.

The so-called Sibylline Books were said to have contained the oracular utterances of a Sibyl or prophetess

1. Pythagoras may have imbibed this doctrine from the Buddhist
East. For a modern revival of it, the reader is referred to P. D.
Ouspensky's great work, *A New Model of the Universe*.

2. J. Carcopino, in his penetrating study, *Virgile et le Mystère de la
IV Eglogue*, finds a source in Pythagoreanism for every concept that
Virgil has embodied in his poem.

who operated from Cumae in Southern Italy in the 6th century B.C. – the place and time in which the Pythagorean philosophy developed. The original books had been destroyed before Virgil's birth, but more or less plausible reconstructions of their contents were current in his day. Besides, he was an antiquary, and we have already seen that he knew enough of the books to use them as his authority for predicting the end of the Iron Age. Is it likely, either that his knowledge stopped here, or that the books themselves did not proceed to state that a new Golden Age would follow? If they did so, it is highly probable that they connected the change of era with the birth of a Wonder-child, if only because Virgil enlarges on this part of the theme, and the later imitations[1] of the older books, which we possess in part, do much the same. The poet, then, seized on this striking idea, and by way of complimenting his friend Pollio was bold enough to foretell that the new age would dawn in his consulship. It is true that he does not explicitly state that the Child too will be born in that year, but he suggests it; and the deceptive appearance of precision in the forecast lends weight and content to the promises which he triumphantly makes to a world that has long been tortured by civil strife.

So far so good; but if we consider Virgil to have deliberately committed himself, if only in his own mind, to the birth of a particular child and to a pair of contemporary parents, our difficulties begin. I will not

1. At the risk of confusing the reader, I must not disguise the fact that there were many 'Sibyls' in the ancient world, and several sets of Sibylline Oracles, including one of Jewish origin, which Virgil may possibly have known. This 'orientation' of Virgil's prophecy is discussed by W. W. Tarn in the *Journal of Roman Studies*, XXII (1932).

weary the reader by passing in review and separately
dismissing all the baby candidates, born and unborn,
who have been nominated for the place of honour.
There are grave objections to all of them, including a
child of Pollio[1] himself, who do not qualify by being
the offspring of one of the two rulers of the Roman
world when Virgil wrote, namely Octavian and
Antony. The wording of the poem demands that the
Child's father shall have pacified the world. Influential
as he was, Pollio had scarcely done that. Only Octavian,
and perhaps Antony, could be described in such terms.
Each of these took a new wife in the year of the poem –
Octavian married Scribonia, and Antony married
Octavian's sister Octavia. The dates would thus fit in
either case, if we allow Virgil to have written rather
late in 40 B.C., and do not press him too hard when he
anticipates by informing the mother that the ten long
months have come to an end. It is true that Antony,
as all Rome knew, had for some time been far too
much preoccupied with Cleopatra in the East to be a
very suitable recipient of such honours from Virgil.
But he qualifies, none the less, through his marriage to
Octavia.[2] Moreover, the field is narrowed still further
in favour of these two great men by another passage
in the poem. When Virgil addresses the Child as 'dear
offspring of the gods, great increment of Jove', it is
hard to believe that he is not thinking of the great

1. Carcopino, in the work I have already cited, ingeniously over-
comes these objections and elects for a son of Pollio. E. K. Rand (in
The Magical Art of Virgil, 1931) comes to much the same conclusion.
2. Some scholars think we have here a wedding-hymn written for
this marriage. It contains echoes from a comparable poem by Catullus;
but I do not agree with D. A. Slater (*Classical Review*, XXVI, 1912)
in his deduction that Antony and Octavia are the pair.

Julian line, the family with which they were both connected, and which was officially credited with a divine
origin (from Jove through Venus), and already boasted
of at least one god, the deified Julius Caesar.

On the whole, then, everything points to Octavian,
with Antony as runner-up. But why, if Virgil wished
to designate either of these men as the father of the
babe, did he not do so? Why are we met with deliberate ambiguity at every point where we attempt to pin
him down? For several reasons. First because Virgil is
Virgil, and that is his way of writing poetry. Secondly
because he did not care to risk the ridicule he might
have incurred had the boy-child of his prophecy turned
out to be a girl.[1] And lastly because, writing in 40 B.C.,
he did not know that the long duel between Octavian
and Antony was to end in Antony's total eclipse and
the establishment of Augustus as undisputed head of
the state. He would not have dared to name either of
the two for fear of offending the other. He was forced
by the circumstances, this time, to 'set a trap for
scholars' – a trap we fall into when we ransack the
poem for convincing clues. He has hinted that he
meant no one in particular, by making it impossible
either for his contemporaries or for us to decide whom
he meant. And incidentally he succeeded in writing a
prophecy which, in spite of its deceptive air of precision, there was no need for him ever to revise or
withdraw. Thus, in the end, it seems that the political
interpretation of the poem approaches much nearer to
the lyrical than might have been expected.

1. It did, in the case of Octavian and Scribonia. Their daughter, Julia,
subsequently so notorious, was born in 39.

III

But there are some who have been dissatisfied with either reading of the poem, and have been led by its real or superficial resemblances to the style of Old Testament prophecy to suggest that Virgil derived his inspiration from Jewish literature. I myself am more impressed by the differences than by the likeness between Virgil and Isaiah. Nor have we any valid reason other than this probably accidental resemblance for supposing that Virgil had so much as heard Isaiah's name. He was certainly a very learned young man, and well-read in the literature of Alexandria, where the Old Testament was translated into Greek. We cannot prove that he did not have access to the Septuagint version or that he had not talked with friends in Rome or Naples who knew it. But I think we can say that, if he did come across the Messianic scriptures and feel inspired by them, he decoded their message very badly. Nothing could be less spiritual, in the Biblical sense, than his material, though at the same time idyllic, conception of the Golden Age. And, as we have seen, he had plenty of material at hand to help him make a Roman oracle.

But in saying this I am by no means rejecting the Christian explanation of the poem which we come to now in our survey. The Church, as it gained strength in Rome, was quick to claim Virgil as one of nature's Christians before the time of Christ. When the Emperor Constantine in the 4th century established Christianity as the state religion, he identified the Child of Virgil's prophecy with Christ; and much later Dante made it clear that he regards Virgil as the next best thing to a Christian. But the acceptance of Constantine's view does not oblige us to prove or even to imagine that Virgil had any direct contact with Jewish literature. It asks far more of us than that. It asks us to believe that Virgil had himself been visited by a prevision of the birth of Christ and had translated his revelation in terms natural to a poet writing as a Roman some forty years before that momentous event. He had seen through a glass darkly – but he had seen.

Of this theory I will only say that we know too little of the human mind and are still too ignorant of the real nature of time for any wise man to dismiss it as absurd. If we are startled by it into thinking unaccustomed thoughts, so much the better. At all events, the very fact that men so notable and so far apart in time or temperament as St Augustine, Constantine, Dante and Alexander Pope concur in blessing it, should teach us to impose no limit on the breadth and depth of meaning we may look to find in Virgil's poetry.

I have attempted to hold the scales fairly through a long series of arguments, and I must now give my own conclusions. For me, the three interpretations have merged into one, without losing their individual validity. The Fourth Eclogue is a lyrical rhapsody. It is a Roman oracle too. It is also a vision, conditioned by its date, but influenced none the less by those mysterious forces which, even as Virgil wrote, were gathering strength in Palestine to shape the future of mankind.

*

V

DAPHNIS AT HEAVEN'S GATE

'He is a portion of the loveliness
Which once he made more lovely.'
Shelley, *Adonais*

IT would be pleasant to dwell on the charm and
subtleties of the Fifth Eclogue; to point out with what
tact the youthful Mopsus secures the comfortable seat
he wants, and how handsomely Menalcas atones for
his unhappy reference to Amyntas; or to enlarge on
the lyrical beauty of the songs that emerge from the
friendly challenge. For in no other Eclogue has Virgil
given more perfect expression to his feeling of the
intimate kinship of man and beast and rock.

But even though I hope the reader will have detected
these qualities in the poem for himself, I am pretty sure
that the first question he will ask is, 'Who is Daphnis?'
We have met him as a handsome swain in the Second
Eclogue; in the Third as a boy who has had his bow
and arrows smashed by Menalcas (now his worshipper);
in the Seventh he is old enough to preside at a singing-
match; and in the Eighth we see him again, as the
recalcitrant lover whom only witchcraft can induce to
abandon the pleasures of the town. But here he seems
to be a god.

The answer is that in this poem Virgil does indeed
kill Daphnis, the ideal country lad and hero of the
Sicilian shepherd fraternity – as Theocritus did before
him. But he goes further and imagines his enrolment
among the minor gods of Olympus as the special
patron of the pastoral community whose ornament he

had been in life, thus transcending the usual limits of the rather obscure Greek story of Daphnis's life and death. And I can only suggest that he does so because he is a poet, and an original one, who felt it an integral part of his task to write the lovely song of praise he has put into Menalcas's mouth, in which an ideal shepherd, by triumphing over death, establishes for ever the unity of man with the living universe that surrounds him.

For me this is enough. But I know very well that from ancient times to the present day other lovers of Virgil have found very good reasons for thinking that, under the disguise of Daphnis, Virgil is lamenting the recent death of a beloved contemporary. I am not referring to Tenney Frank's theory[1] that this was the poet Cornificius – there is little evidence to support this attractive view; nor to the suggestion that Virgil is mourning for a brother called Flaccus – no sensible poet would think he was doing an obscure relative a service by attempting to promote him to Olympus at one stroke of the pen; but to the more tenable theory that this apotheosis of Daphnis is to be read as the counterpart of the recent official deification of the dictator Julius Caesar.

Unfortunately, to my way of thinking, everything appears at first sight to favour the allegorizers here. It all fits in very neatly. The 'cruel death' suits Caesar's end almost better than that of Daphnis; Caesar (according to Servius) did introduce Bacchic rites into Italy; Daphnis's 'lovely flock' is readily identifiable with the Roman people; Daphnis had 'loved Menalcas too', and Caesar had specially favoured Virgil's homeland

1. Put forward by him in *Vergil, A Biography* (1922).

in Cisalpine Gaul – and so on. The facts that Daphnis died as a lad, and Caesar as an elderly man with a bald head; that Daphnis's mother is alive to mourn him, whereas Caesar's had died many years before her son was assassinated; that 'the good Daphnis stands for peace', whereas Caesar had been fighting for the last sixteen years of his life, and incidentally had cut off the hands of every man who resisted him in Uxellodunum – all these and other trifling incongruities are lightly brushed aside. And indeed, as Professor H. J. Rose says in his *Handbook of Latin Literature*, with Octavian in power it was quite in order for Virgil, or anyone else, to praise his "father" Julius Caesar to the skies. But this does not prove that Virgil does so here. And we might well ask why, if he was at liberty to laud Caesar openly, he has adopted this baffling camouflage for his admiration.

Let me confess that I am conscious of some prejudice in arguing the case against the allegory. But prejudice is the hardest thing to avoid in literary judgments. And I not only feel this to be a question of good taste, but would go so far as to say that a lovely poem is spoilt for me, when the dead Dictator is dragged on to the stage. My feelings towards Julius Caesar have not been left unaffected by recent events in Europe. However, Virgil was not an Englishman; there is much to show that he did make a hero of Caesar; and I must not allow myself to promote topical reactions to the status of an argument. Let us see whether we have no stouter weapons to rely on.

I spoke just now of good taste. We are dealing with some of the best poetry of a first-rate poet, who may sometimes have written with speed but certainly did not publish in careless haste. His caprice in repeatedly using the same names for different characters in his book must be quite conscious and deliberate.[1] We have already found Daphnis appearing elsewhere in the *Eclogues* in four capacities, none of which tallies very well with his mythological status in the Fifth, still less with his supposed rôle as Julius Caesar – and we cannot complain. It is Virgil's way; and perhaps none of the duplications amounts to absolute incongruity. But a fifth and worse case remains to be examined.

In the year after Julius Caesar's death, Octavian gave a spectacle in his adoptive father's honour. During the games, and in full daylight, we are told that a 'star', which was probably a comet, made its appearance in the sky and was hailed as the soul of Caesar on its way to heaven. In the Ninth Eclogue, Virgil advises a shepherd to adjust his calendar by this newly-risen light, the star of Caesar – and *Daphnis* is that shepherd's name. In fact, if the allegory in the Fifth Eclogue is to stand, Daphnis, alive, is told in the Ninth to watch his own departing soul in its ascent to Olympus. This is worse than incongruous. I find it hard to believe that Virgil was guilty of such inadvertence.

That is my case. But I may be wrong; and I have most of the scholars against me. At all events I shall continue to draw a sharp distinction in my own mind between Daphnis as the darling of the countryside and Daphnis the Conqueror of Gaul.

1. A glance at the Glossary will show the reader what I mean. At the same time, I must admit that it has been argued that every name in the *Eclogues* represents one and always the same person. See Léon Herrmann, *Les Masques et les Visages dans les Bucoliques de Virgile* (Bruxelles, 1930).

VI

THE SONG OF SILENUS

'Then, with a shout, we leapt upon him and flung our
arms round his back.'

Homer, Odyssey, IV

THE Sixth Eclogue can be read and enjoyed in an
entirely non-controversial spirit. Yet, apart from its
charm, the poem, which like the Fourth deals with a
somewhat loftier theme than the rest, contains several
points that challenge attention. The dedication itself
is one of these. Virgil's choice of his legendary material
is another. And a third (closely connected with the
second) is the curious manner in which his friend
Gallus is suddenly brought into the picture.

To begin, then, with the introductory lines – we are
not certain who this Varus was. Servius thinks he was
the Publius Alfenus Varus who was entrusted with the
allotment of lands to Octavian's soldiers, and confiscated Virgil's farm – or else did not. But we have
already seen good reason to doubt the several variations of this tale, and our doubts are intensified when
we read on the same page the alternative suggestion
that he was Publius Quinctilius Varus, who, some fifty
years *after* this Eclogue was composed, lost three
legions for Augustus in the depths of Germany. Who-
ever Varus was, and whatever the poet's obligation to
him may have been, Virgil disposes of any hopes he
may have entertained of having his achievements sung
by his friend, as adroitly as he does for Pollio in the
Eighth Eclogue, and even more firmly. The interesting
point is that, while thus excusing himself from writing

contemporary epic, Virgil gives us a straightforward account, in the first person, of his past and future plans for poetical work. He tells us that he is going to devote himself to rural melodies; the impulse that inspired the *Eclogues* is not yet exhausted, nor are the *Georgics* yet conceived. All there remains for us to ask is who were the kings and what the battles that he once had thought of making his theme. Is this an intimation that he had already imagined an *Aeneid* and rejected the plan, only to resume it in later life; or had some other historical epic for a short time occupied his attention? Tenney Frank thinks he had actually begun the *Aeneid* by the time he wrote this Eclogue, indeed before Julius Caesar's death. But Servius accepts the second explanation and tells us that the young Virgil began a poem about the kings of Alba Longa (the mother-city of Rome), but abandoned the project on account of the harshness of their names – an objection to which the god of poetry had no doubt given due weight before he touched the poet's ear.

Apart from the dedication, the poem itself tells us interesting things about Virgil's inward history. The account of the creation with which Silenus opens his song is a summary of that given by the Epicurean philosopher Lucretius in his great poem *The Nature of the Universe*. Elsewhere Virgil refers more than once to his own early and persistent interest in philosophy, and by repeated references to Lucretius and echoes from his work makes it obvious how much he was indebted to the older poet, though he never mentions him by name.

I myself feel that Virgil's interest in Epicurus is sufficient reason for the prominence he gives in the

Eclogue to this piece of Epicurean philosophy. But its
inclusion caused Servius (or maybe one of his predecessors) to put forward the theory that, under the
alias of Silenus, Virgil is recalling or even parodying
the teaching of his tutor Siro, the Epicurean lecturer
at whose feet both he and Varus had sat. Tenney Frank
for once agrees with him and joins the allegorizers. Yet
the more I read the poem, the more alien do I find its
mood to the spirit of parody, allegory, or anything but
straightforward and transparent poetry. I am quite
convinced that we should be wrong in depriving
Silenus of his purely mythological status.

Of this, there is not much to be said. Silenus was one
of the minor figures of the Greek pantheon, a satyr-
like attendant on Dionysus, the god of wine. In this
passage at least, he bears a curious resemblance to
Proteus, the Old Man of the Sea, whose story as given
us by Homer I refer to at the head of this essay. The
old reprobate was evidently a consummate artist, and
we must look leniently on his morals. But Conington's
scruples are not so easily appeased. He takes so sinister
a view of the 'reward' Silenus had in mind for Aegle
that he omits the whole passage from his translation.
Servius, who lived too soon to benefit by the example
of Dr Bowdler, takes a very different and even more
amusing line. After assisting the dull student by filling
in the blank, he commends Virgil's modesty for leaving something unexpressed.

The poet's choice and handling of the tales included
in Silenus's repertory have been much discussed and
have come under heavy fire from Victorian scholars.
I quote only the patronizing and subtly disparaging
remark of T. E. Page: 'The Epicurean theory of crea-

tion and the myths which follow are merely regarded
by Virgil as both affording material for the display of
his poetic skill.' Might we not with equal propriety
compliment Homer, Dante and Shakespeare on their
adroitness in choosing the themes best adapted to
their not inconsiderable talents? Why not give Virgil
credit for a genuine interest in his material, whatever
caused him to select it, and enjoy the artistry with
which he has handled each well-known tale and caught
its most picturesque moment in a few masterly words?
All I can find to blame him for is the trouble he has put
me to in supplementing his brevity for the benefit of
such readers as may care to consult my glossary. In one
case, indeed, he has made my task impossible, by not
even giving us Atalanta's name; and I seize this
occasion to explain that she was a swift-footed maiden
whose suitors had to beat her in a race or die. In the
end she was won by Milanion, who had the fore-
thought to provide himself with three golden apples
and throw them at her feet as she outstripped him.

But perhaps there *is* some cause for comment, even
for surprise, when, in the midst of this mythological
cavalcade, we come upon a living man, the poet Gallus.
Conington finds 'great incongruity' here. Servius, less
prone to criticize where he does not understand, suggests indebtedness to Gallus on Virgil's part and once
more brings up the old story of the evictions and the
confiscated farm. Virgil may perhaps have been
indebted to Gallus; but what is far more to the point
in explaining this passage is the fact that Gallus was a
fellow-poet, that Virgil loved him dearly, and that he
wholeheartedly admired his work. It has been thought
likely that, if we had Gallus's poems before us and

could re-read the Eclogue in their light, all would be
clear and the abruptness of his appearance on the stage
would be removed. The German scholar F. Skutsch[1]
went so far as to argue with great ingenuity and learn-
ing that the various episodes covered by Silenus's song
form a sort of synopsis of one or more of Gallus's
works. It is indeed an attractive thought that some
gleams from these lost jewels may filter through to us
not only in the last Eclogue but in this one also. Yet it
is difficult to believe that Virgil composed a poem con-
sisting for by far the greater part of a mere *resumé* of
the recent work of a living poet; and I myself prefer
to seek the clue in the final paragraph of the
Eclogue, and ask whether Virgil himself is not referring us to his source (just as he does in the Fourth
Eclogue), when he tells us that Silenus gave the two
lads the same songs as the fortunate Eurotas had once
heard from Apollo's lips. If we could discover an
earlier Greek poet who had handled this theme at
length, I think our quest for Virgil's sources would be
at an end. Nor would his use of such material from
a Greek poem entail anything to surprise us.

However that may be, I find this undisguised and
temporary 'apotheosis' of Gallus much easier to swallow than the alleged apotheosis of Julius Caesar under
the alias of Daphnis in the Fifth Eclogue. Moreover,
as we shall see when we come to the Tenth, it was not
beyond Virgil's whimsical genius to experiment still
more boldly with his friend and to picture him in far
more embarrassing scenes than this.

What *is* intriguing is that this high compliment
should have been paid to Gallus in a poem that Virgil

1. *Aus Vergils Frühzeit* (1901) and *Gallus und Vergil* (1906).

dedicates, not without a good measure of conventional flattery, to Varus. However, we know too little of the relationships that obtained between the three men to explain away this apparent anomaly; and Varus's position in the trio remains obscure. But an interesting sidelight is thrown on the literary coterie to which Virgil and Gallus belonged, and of which we get tantalizing glimpses here and there in the *Eclogues*, by a delightful story in Servius, which I should in any case have quoted for its own sake. Of its authenticity I shall say nothing more than that the date of Cicero's death, in 43 B.C., makes it just possible that the tale is as true as it is good.

According to Servius, then, Virgil's recitations of this Eclogue impressed his friends so favourably[1] that they decided to put it on the stage, and it was sung by the actress Cythēris, whom we meet under the name of Lycōris as Gallus's mistress in the last Eclogue. Cicero, attending one of these performances, was so much captivated[2] that he asked who had written the words, and on securing an introduction to the young poet, hailed him as 'Rome's second hope', thereby paying himself as great a compliment as Virgil.

1. No wonder, if Skutsch is right. Gallus would of course take kindly to so effective an advertisement of his own poetry.

2. Servius uses the same word, *stupefactus*, as Virgil does in VIII when describing the mental condition of the lynxes who listened to the music of Damon and Alphesiboeus.

VII

THE SINGING-MATCH

'I've a grand memory for forgetting.'
R. L. Stevenson

HERE we have another strictly amoebaean contest, like that of the Third Eclogue, except that the singers are given four lines each instead of two in every round. Another and more significant difference is that this time the result is not a dead-heat but a decisive victory for one of the performers. This means that Virgil has once more set himself a delicate task. If the poems he puts into Thyrsis's mouth do not prove inferior to those of Corydon, we shall be left with the feeling that injustice has been done to the loser; while, if they are to be inferior, Virgil must deliberately lower his standard when writing for Thyrsis. It has amused critics to attempt to decide how the poet escapes from this dilemma.

Actually it is very hard to detect any drop in level marked enough to justify the resounding victory that Corydon is allowed to score. [1] The unfortunate Thyrsis is, of course, handicapped from the very start by being given the second place – a severe disadvantage, as I pointed out in my essay on the Third Eclogue. As a result, less pleasing themes are forced upon him more than once. When Corydon sings of spring, what can Thyrsis do but fall back on the alleviations of winter? Yet he acquits himself well, and I am inclined to think

1. Professor H. J. Rose is most ingenious in detecting a number of slight blemishes in Thyrsis's style (*The Eclogues of Vergil*, 1942, pp. 145–147).

that it is a difference of character between the two shepherd-poets, rather than a contrast between their artistic achievements, that Virgil intends us to detect. In the first round, for instance, Corydon not only combines with modesty a laudable degree of ambition, but shows himself to be a generous friend, whereas Thyrsis alienates our sympathies by an excess of self-confidence. Again, in the second round, Priapus might well take umbrage, not so much at the quantity and quality of his perquisites as at the mercenary and disrespectful attitude of his devotee. Nor, if he is wise, will the little scarecrow god place much reliance on the promise of a golden statue – that is sheer bombast. Indeed, one feels that in Thyrsis's garden he is lucky to be made of marble, not of wood; and that, if things go wrong with the flock, he will certainly be as roundly blamed as the Wine-god is, in a later quatrain, for the parching of the vines.

However, if this difference in amiability between the two lads is not enough, we may be sure that Virgil, with his usual cunning, has left himself a loophole to escape by. Meliboeus's excellent memory carries him through six rounds of the contest without a hitch, and then fails completely, long before the knock-out blow is delivered by Corydon. If, up to this moment, equal points have been scored, and neither Thyrsis nor Virgil has disgraced himself, it must be afterwards, in the unreported rounds, which we shall never hear, that we must imagine Thyrsis, though putting up a gallant show, to weaken gradually, and to take the final count. In fact, Meliboeus's memory fails because Virgil himself has failed in the attempt to write inferior verse.

Apart from this intriguing puzzle, the only difficulties that the poem presents are minute or imaginary. We have already learnt enough of Virgil's way with geography to feel no surprise when we find a couple of Arcadian lads driving down their flocks to the banks of 'Smooth-sliding Mincius, crowned with vocal reeds'. If taxed on this point, Virgil might well have replied that they were Arcadian in their spirit and accomplishments. It is certainly in this non-geographical sense that the phrase 'Arcadians both' became a catchword with our ancestors, though I am at a loss to explain why and when it assumed its disparaging tone.[1]

Servius, in commenting on the Eclogue, falls once more into an allegorizing mood. We are not only faced with the possibility that Daphnis may be Caesar again, but we are invited to think that Virgil, assuming yet another alias, is Corydon here. From this, it is an easy step to identify the defeated Thyrsis with the Mevius or Bavius whom Virgil has held up to ridicule in the Third Eclogue – we can take our choice. Codrus too becomes a living poet, though a better one, for whom Servius quotes a contemporary sponsor named Valgius.

This is all very well, and indeed, for all we know, there may be references here to the literary coterie I have already spoken of. But once one starts allegorizing it is difficult to stop, and Servius carries things to the point of absurdity when he suggests that the Daphnis of this Eclogue is once more the divine being that Virgil makes of him in the Fifth, because it took a god to assure Meliboeus of the safety not only of his wandering billy-goat but of his kids as well. We, bringing our mortal intellect to bear on the problem, find

1. Maybe Byron was responsible, when he wrote: ' "Arcades ambo" id est – blackguards both'. *Don Juan*, canto IV, xciii.

no difficulty in supposing that the kids had followed
their runaway senior, as kids do, and that Daphnis had
spied the whole party, with Meliboeus in chase not far
behind them.

VIII

DAMON AND ALPHESIBOEUS

'Lynxes do not exist in Italy.'

T. E. Page

'One of the least successful of the Eclogues.'

R. C. Trevelyan

THE Eighth Eclogue is prefaced by as elaborate an introduction as the Sixth, but this time it is to Pollio, not to Varus, that Virgil excuses himself for preferring the pastoral to the narrative muse. It is true that he does not mention Pollio by name, as he does when he compliments him so highly in the Fourth; also that Servius for some reason takes it for granted that he means Octavian, not Pollio. But the dates and references fit Pollio best, and it is generally accepted that he is the person meant. Both before and after his consulship in 40 B.C. he was in the north, and in 39 he had been despatched on a punitive expedition against a Dalmatian tribe, and so might aptly be imagined by Virgil as passing the mouth of the River Timavus in Venetia and sailing down the Adriatic Sea on his triumphant return from his mission. Moreover, he is known to have written tragedies, though we do not possess them and cannot tell to what extent they merited the praise which Virgil and Horace[1] bestow on them.

The singing-match recorded in the poem itself is not really amoebaean, but more like the friendly exchange of songs that we have had in the Fifth Eclogue. There is no umpire, no decision between the rival per-

1. Odes, II. 1.

formers; both sing of love, but there is no deliberate contrast in their ways of handling the theme; and the two songs do not even correspond exactly in their structure.

Many modern editors are at pains to point out how much Virgil owes to Theocritus throughout the poem and particularly in the second half. They also sprinkle their notes with the word 'artificial', and T. E. Page gives some precision to his use of this ambiguous and maltreated term by such remarks as 'Lynxes do not exist in Italy, but the whole scene is imaginary'; to which the only adequate reply is, 'Exactly so'. I have already tilted, in the Introduction, against these misconceptions of the poet's aims. I could go further and cite Voltaire and Macaulay on the other side. But in questions of taste, especially in deciding where artifice comes in and art goes out, every reader must be his own authority. Those who love Virgil love this poem. For them its 'artificiality' is art. Others may fall back on that useful word to crystallize their disapproval of a thing not fully understood.

A few words on the witchcraft poem. The theme is taken from an Idyl by Theocritus, with many a change, including the happy ending. But it is not these differences between the two poets to which I wish to draw attention, so much as the ubiquity and persistence of magic ceremonial and procedure. What satisfied Greek readers as sound witchcraft in the 3rd century B.C., and Romans in the 1st, would have passed muster in Jacobean England, and scarcely needs a note to-day. Religions come and go: magic, for the most part, remains the same. I have verified my impression that to this day there are folk in England who stick pins

into effigies[1] of people they dislike. The methods
Amaryllis used are only a little more elaborate, and, for
all I know, they may yet be in vogue.

Moeris, of course, must have been an exceptionally
powerful sorcerer, if Amaryllis does not overstate his
claims. As a practising werewolf, he contrasts very
oddly with his namesake in the next Eclogue, a dis-
illusioned elderly shepherd who is no match for wolves.
As for his further accomplishments, no spiritualist
should boggle at the claim that he could call up ghosts
from deep down in the grave. And if some sceptic
should object that the shifting of a standing crop is an
even more formidable undertaking, I should refer him
to the excellent Servius, who tells us that such things
were actually done. At any rate there was a law against
them in the Twelve Tables. Which goes some way to
prove the attempt, if not the deed.

When I spoke just now of Amaryllis's magic technique, I begged the question whether two people are
involved in this dramatic scene or only one – in addi-
tion of course to Daphnis, who arrives just after the
curtain has dropped. The usual interpretation (indeed
the only one I have seen) is that two are present, the
unnamed wife as chief performer, and a servant called
Amaryllis, as assistant. But Virgil leaves us quite free
to regard the song as a monologue, with Amaryllis
addressing admonitions to herself. I feel that this
interpretation heightens the effect.

It has also been disputed whether Damon, when
singing his song, leans against the trunk of an olive-
tree or on a staff of olive-wood – Virgil merely says 'a

1. 'Mommets', as they are called, owing, originally, to a false idea
that idols of Mahomet were made by his followers.

smooth olive'. Much has been written in this connection about the gnarled and rugged habit of the olive-
tree, and of the discomfort of leaning against it. Much
could also be said about the difficulty of playing a pipe
with one hand otherwise occupied. I prefer to leave
Damon with both hands free for his instrument, and
to think that, if olive-trunks are mostly rough, that is
the reason why Virgil took the trouble to tell us that
Damon chose a smooth one for his back. His thought
for the comfort of the shepherd is as characteristic as
his concern for the satisfaction of the flock. It is Virgil
at his best to take the sheep's view of the beauty of the
morning dew on the grass.

To conclude, Servius, as usual, has a good story to
tell us. It concerns Cicero once more; in fact it is taken
from the poem he wrote in honour of his own achievements as consul in the year 63 B.C. His wife had just
sacrificed and was about to pour a drink-offering on
the ashes, when these burst into flame, just as they did
for Amaryllis. This meant – it is not stated why – that
Cicero would be elected consul in the same year.
And he was.

E

IX

THE ROAD TO TOWN

Two countrymen meet on the way to town and fall into conversation. One of them, Moeris, has just been evicted from his holding to make place for a veteran – we have come upon a comparable scene in the First Eclogue. His companion, Lycidas, who is behind-hand with the news, recalls the endeavour of a fellow-farmer, Menalcas, who is something of a poet, to save the district from this legalized brigandage by a petition in verse to the authorities. But Moeris is able to inform him of the failure of this move, and dwells on the dangers that Menalcas underwent in his attempt. The pair then while away the time by reciting such verses as they can remember from the poems of their friend.

This sounds simple, and read in this way, which is the way I recommend to the English reader, the poem *is* simple, as well as delightful. Unfortunately, the topical allusions it contains are so suggestively precise, and yet, when scrutinized, so vague, as to leave room for a flood of speculation. Moreover, the poem bears certain affinities to an Idyl of the Greek pastoral poet Theocritus which has been shown to bristle with camouflaged references to real people, and, although it is always dangerous to argue from Theocritus to Virgil, since Virgil is nowhere more original than in his 'imitations', the net result is that we are faced once more, and in an even acuter form, with the questions already touched on in discussing the First Eclogue: 'Does Virgil mean us to take the poet Menalcas for himself, and is it his own farm and the loss of it that he is deploring?'

Let me assure the reader at once that I am not going to take him far, this time, down the labyrinthine ways of hypothesis, allegory and reconstruction. My feeling is that if Virgil set out to make the poem autobiographical (which I do not believe), he for some reason so obscured the clues as to defeat his purpose, possibly because he still felt himself on dangerous ground, but still more probably because the instincts of a poet overruled the first intentions of a reporter. All we are left to say is that the poem seems too factual to pass as completely imaginary, and that Menalcas may well stand for some actual farmer-poet who made an appeal to Varus, one of the commissioners, when the lands of Cremona had been seized and those of its neighbour Mantua were threatened. But the identification of Menalcas with Virgil is not proven (in spite of his last speech in the Fifth Eclogue): there is nothing to compel us to the belief that Virgil devoted a whole eclogue to the praise of his own poetry.

I am not denying that those who accept the identification, and chase the elusive clues, put themselves in the way of some excellent sport. Indeed the hunt becomes exciting at as early a point as Lycidas's second speech, where, if Menalcas is Virgil, we may well feel that we are listening to the poet's description of his own ancestral farm. Scholars have even visited the locality in the hope of identifying the spot. No excursion could be more enjoyable. But the reports they bring back are unconvincing – as anyone who has studied the poet's evasive technique might have foretold. Moreover, as T. E. Page and E. K. Rand have pointed out, Lycidas is surely describing a district, not a single farm.[1]

In the snatches of song that Virgil causes the two friends to quote from Menalcas's works, we certainly seem to be offered clues, but the scent of the red herring is strong in the air. These lines are not quotations from the other Eclogues. If they are Virgil's (and they sound like his) he either wrote them for insertion in this work or has taken them from poems of his own that he did not include for publication in his final selection. Actually he has left us quite free to regard them as extracts from the work of a fellow-poet – one of the 'singing swans' of Mantua, perhaps – whom he disguises under the Greek name of Menalcas. But I do not stress that possibility so much as the care that Virgil used, if he did write the verses himself, to prevent his 'Menalcas' from being caught in the act of quoting Virgil and so enabling us to clinch the identification of the two. He has even gone to the trouble, in the first quotation, of making Menalcas give orders to Tityrus (that useful factotum who seems always at hand to look after other people's goats), in spite of the fact that in the Sixth Eclogue he identifies Tityrus with himself. If some case-hardened allegorizer insists, nevertheless, on making Virgil say, 'Feed my goats, Virgil, while I am gone' – my sympathies go out to the goats.

The three lines addressed to Varus throw no light on the problem of Menalcas's identity. If a poetical appeal *was* made, we are left to guess who made it, as well as

1. An interesting discussion of the problem is given by R. S. Conway in *The Vergilian Age* (1928), to which reference has already been made in the Essay on I (p. 89).

what effect it had. The allusion to the unfinished state
of the poem even suggests the possibility that this very
Eclogue is itself the famous appeal and the only one
that was ever penned.

But there is a point at which conjecture becomes
futile; and with the third quotation we happily pass
from controversial ground. The Galatea here addressed
defeats all attempts to convert her into anyone but her
delightful self. It is only to be observed that she is not
the country wench who had jilted Tityrus in the First
Eclogue, but a sea-nymph whom the Cyclops Polyphemus loved.

The fourth song is equally clear of complexities. It
is an undisguised tribute to the deified Julius Caesar.
I gave some account of the celestial phenomenon that
Virgil recalls, when I cited these lines in my essay on
the Fifth Eclogue as evidence against the allegorical
interpretation of that poem. Servius rounds off the tale
by telling us that Octavian had a golden star placed
above the head of his adoptive father when he erected
a statue of him in the Capitol.

In the dialogue of the poem there is one point that
may strike the reader as odd. I refer to the sudden
appearance of two 'real' poets, Cinna and Varius, and
the praise that Virgil causes Moeris to bestow on them.
We know something of these men, and Virgil's contemporaries knew more. One of them, Cinna, a great
friend of the poet Catullus, had been killed in mistake
for a namesake while walking in Caesar's funeral procession. The other, Varius, lived to become one of
Virgil's literary executors. Here they stand out undisguised, like islands in the misty seas of camouflaged
allusion. I take this as a pretty strong hint that when

Virgil wants to talk openly about someone he does so, and that for the rest, his allusions to living people, if any, are made deliberately unintelligible, except, maybe, to the literary circle of which he was a member.

I have after all got myself so deeply involved in the intriguing speculations to which the poem invites us that I have left its praises unsung. I see that Servius too is so much preoccupied with the task of reconstructing history from fiction, that he has little space left for his usual titbits of information and enlightenment. He does tell us, however, how Moeris came to lose his voice. It is one of the things that happen to a man when the wolves spy him before he spies the wolves. 'Even the physicians,' he says, 'confirm the truth of this.'

X

GALLUS

'Who would not sing for *Lycidas*? he knew
Himself to sing, and build the lofty rhyme.'

Milton

'What would we not barter of all the epics of the Empire
for a few pages written by Gallus?'

Tenney Frank

No one whom Virgil loved as he loved Gallus could fail to attract us. And Gallus has other claims than these on our affection. Here, briefly, is what we know about this remarkable man.

Gaius Cornelius Gallus was born at Forum Julii (now Fréjus) in Southern Gaul a year or so after Virgil. His parents were humble folk, but it would be wrong to assume that they were Gauls on account of the name – it was one that several distinguished Romans had already borne. However, those who know Fréjus and the neighbouring mountains of the Esterel on the Riviera are free to interpret his character in whatever terms of early Celtic influence they may care to imagine.

He must have come to Rome while still a lad, for we are told that he had published a volume of poems by the time he was twenty. He seems to have attracted Julius Caesar's attention and is reported to have studied philosophy with Virgil under Siro. But, unlike Virgil, he had political, as well as literary, ambitions, and, by the time we meet him in the *Eclogues*, he had become a trusted lieutenant of Octavian and had been appointed one of the Commissioners for the redistribution of lands in Northern Italy.

The poems of Gallus that Virgil refers to as having

been composed in 'Chalcidic verse' were imitations of
Greek originals by the Alexandrine poet Euphorion,
of Chalcis in Euboea. There is good reason for thinking that these were not identical with the four books
of love poems that Gallus is known to have dedicated
to his mistress Lycōris. It seems clear, at all events,
that it was Gallus's intimate and self-revealing treat-
ment of the theme of love which placed him among the
foremost Roman elegists, inspired the regretful admiration of Propertius after his death, and caused Ovid to
say that he and his Lycōris would be read from the
rising to the setting sun.

But Gallus does not appear to have followed up this
early literary success. The soldier and statesman in him
overcame the poet, and when next he gave rein to his
exuberant fancy, it was in another direction and with
tragic results.

He continued for many years to serve Octavian with
distinction. At the decisive battle of Actium in 31 B.C.,
when the fleet of Antony and Cleopatra was routed,
Gallus held a high command. He was entrusted with
the pursuit to Egypt and played a gallant part in the
final operations in that country. The historian Dio
Cassius gives us interesting details, which show us
that the passionate lover could also be a resourceful
and imaginative commander in the field. Gallus cap-
tured a town called Paraetonium, on the coast west of
Alexandria. When Antony came up to the attack,
Gallus was perturbed by the knowledge that he had
in his garrison a number of men who had served with
Antony and might be won over by him if he were
given an opportunity of suborning their loyalty. Gallus
let Antony come right up to the walls, and then, as he

prepared to address the defenders, he ordered all his
trumpeters to sound their instruments together, and to
continue the uproar, with the result that Antony was
forced to retire without having been able to get a word
across.

An assault was made, but it failed, and a naval force
was now detailed to attack the place, which had a
harbour with a very narrow entrance. Gallus drew
chains across this, but left them lying on the bottom,
and avoided the appearance of guarding the spot.
Antony's fleet incautiously seized the opportunity to
sail in during the night. Gallus raised the chains behind
them by mechanical means, and, once he had them
confined in the harbour, destroyed them easily.

In recognition of his services he was now made the
first Prefect or, as we should say, Viceroy of Egypt by
Octavian and distinguished himself by quelling a
rebellion at Thebes. But power had gone to his head
and affected his judgment. Instead of attributing his
successes to the Emperor, as tact and policy demanded,
he claimed the merit for himself, had his own statues
erected everywhere, and even caused self-laudatory
inscriptions to be put on the Pyramids. He had enemies
enough to ensure that such conduct should be reported
at Rome and interpreted as evidence of disloyalty. The
matter was dealt with in the Senate, Gallus was recalled,
and, though not condemned to death by his old friend
Augustus, felt that he had fallen beyond redemption,
and took his own life.[1]

Even his poems seem to have suffered from his dis-

1. Suetonius, in his *Life of Augustus*, reports that the Emperor com-
plained, with tears, that he was the only man who could not set what
limits he chose to his anger with his friends.

grace, and Ovid's prophecy was not fulfilled. There are few references to them later than those I have mentioned. Quintilian, writing a century after his death, knows his works, and Servius appears to know them. After that they are swallowed up in the dark night that closed down on so much that was beautiful in Greek and Roman letters. Even references to Gallus appear to have been discouraged. The Fourth Book of Virgil's *Georgics*, as first composed, is said by Servius[1] to have contained a long story of which Gallus was the hero. His disgrace and death intervened, Augustus objected, and Virgil substituted for the offending passage the beautiful tale of Orpheus and his Eurydice with which the book now closes.

One more misfortune overtook the ill-starred Gallus, and that when he had lain for eighteen centuries in the grave. A German named Becker, setting out to write an informative book on how the Romans lived, made him the clothes-peg of his tale. Many a Victorian schoolboy on a prize-giving day has walked up to the platform in unsuspecting innocence and come away with Becker's *Gallus* on his hands.

Such was the man whom Virgil has immortalized as the first discarded lover to think of big game as an antidote to love. It was a bold experiment to put him in among the sheep and goats and make a lovelorn swain out of the militant statesman of the Civil Wars, though perhaps no bolder than Milton's when he relieved his sorrow for the death of an undergraduate friend by calling on Arcadia for its tears. Scarcely a

1. His statements are dismissed as nonsense by Professor W. B. Anderson (*Classical Quarterly*, XXVII, 1933) and Professor H. J. Rose (*Handbook of Latin Literature*, 1936).

commentator till we come to Tenney Frank has resisted
the lure of the easy label 'artificial', and, though some
have conceded the extraordinary beauty of the poem,
Conington, unconquered to the end, complains that
'the identification of shepherd and poet is so rudely
managed as to amount to absolute confusion'. Now I
will not anticipate the reader's judgment nor spoil his
pleasure by dwelling on the subtlety and elegance of
this tribute from one poet to another. But there is
one clue to its interpretation that all who read the
poem should possess. Conington had it before him, in
his own words, had he but seen it. For 'the identification of shepherd and poet' had already been made,
before Virgil made it, by Gallus himself, in his
Lycōris Elegies.

We owe it to Servius that we can reconstruct the
story. He tells us that many of the words that Virgil
puts into the mouth of Gallus the shepherd are actually
quotations from the works of Gallus the poet. If
Gallus then, on some real or imaginary campaign or on
leave in Greece, had heard that his darling had run off
with another officer and had published his grief in
pastoral vein, what could be more natural than for his
friend Virgil to condole with him in the same idiom?
I will even suggest that Gallus in one of his other
poems had gently twitted Virgil by picturing him
among his sheep and goats, and that this Eclogue is
Virgil's reply, full of the playful tenderness that made
him dear to all his friends.

If this is really so, if half the words and sentiments of
this delightful poem are originally those of Gallus, let
us thank Virgil for preserving them for us, yet with
such tact and skill that no dismemberment or crude

analysis can rob the whole of its unity or make us feel
that we are reading anything but a masterpiece of Virgil's own. I like to think that it really was the future
Viceroy of Egypt who in the pangs of ill-requited love
had had the grace to spare an anxious thought for the
dainty feet of his beloved runaway.

GLOSSARY

GLOSSARY

of legendary, fictional and historical characters and of place-names mentioned in the translation

ACHILLES (IV). The most famous of the Greek captains who took part in the Trojan War; the hero of Homer's *Iliad*. For the significance of Virgil's prophecy about him in IV, see the Essay on that Eclogue.

ADONIS (X). In Greek story Adonis was a beautiful youth fatally loved by Aphrodite, whose outraged husband, Ares, took the form of a wild-boar and killed him. Virgil is here referring to the fact that he was brought up in pastoral surroundings by the Nymphs.

Aphrodite's grief was so great that she secured from Hades permission for Adonis to spend part of each year with her in the upper world. The original cult had reference to the seasonal death and rebirth of vegetation, and one of its special features was the 'Gardens of Adonis', in which flowers were grown round his image. Shakespeare tells part of his tale in *Venus and Adonis*, and a 'Garden of Adonis' figures in Spenser's *Faery Queen* and elsewhere in Elizabethan literature.

AEGLE (VI). A Nymph to whom Virgil attributes a prominent part in the attack on Silenus in VI. The name means 'brilliance' and is thus appropriate to a Naiad or water-sprite.

AEGON (II, V). In II, Aegon is referred to as a sheep-owner and as Menalcas's rival for Neaera's love. In V, however (where he is described as a native of Crete), Menalcas counts on him for a song at the Festival of Daphnis.

AGANIPPE (X). A Naiad, whose spring was situated at the foot of Mt Helicon in the part of Boeotia known as Aonia, and was thus connected with the Muses and poetry.

ALCIMEDON (III). A wood-carver otherwise unknown to us.

ALCIPPE (VII). A farm-girl.

ALCON (V). Here, probably, only a pastoral character, and not the famous archer who accompanied Hercules.

ALEXIS (II, VII). A beautiful lad, loved in II by Corydon and again referred to by him in VII. Suetonius would have us believe that, under the pseudonym of Alexis, Virgil is referring to a friend of his own called Alexander.

ALPHESIBOEUS (V, VIII). Referred to as a champion dancer in V, he sings the witchcraft song in VIII, in competition with Damon.

ALPINE (X). The Alps had no romantic appeal for the Romans. When Gallus feels 'the call of the wild', as he does in X, his thoughts turn to the lower altitudes and milder asperities of Arcadia.

AMARYLLIS (I, II, VIII, IX). In I a country lass in love with Tityrus; in II the rather difficult lady whom Corydon once loved. In the witchcraft song in VIII she lures home her lover, or her husband, Daphnis, by means of magic ritual; and in IX she appears as a general favourite.

AMPHION (II). A mythical hero. In the *Odyssey* (Book XI) he and his brother Zethus are described as the founders of Thebes of the Seven Gates, but Homer does not go on to tell us that when building its walls Amphion played the lyre so beautifully that the stones moved into place of their own accord. Virgil is referring to an earlier stage in the life of this remarkable musician, when he was brought up by shepherds in the mountains of Boeotia.

AMYNTAS (II, III, V, X). A shepherd, mentioned in II as a devotee of the reed-pipe, and in III as a youth dear to Menalcas, who nevertheless, in V, speaks disparagingly of his performance as a musician. In X, Gallus mentions him as a typical country lad, handsome though dark.

ANTIGENES (V). Is referred to by Mopsus as a good-looking boy. There is no reason to identify him (as Servius does) with one of Virgil's friends.

AONIAN (VI, X). Aonia was a part of Boeotia in which

Mt Helicon and the Spring of Aganippe were situated. Thus it was connected with the Muses.

APOLLO. See under *Phoebus Apollo*.

ARACYNTHUS (II). A mountain on the borders of Attica and Boeotia.

ARCADY (IV, VII, X). Arcadia was a mountainous country in the centre of the Peloponnesus, or southern peninsula of Greece. Its idealization by Virgil and subsequent poets has some basis in fact. Its hill-pastures and hunting-grounds supported a mainly rural community; it was the original home of the worship of Pan, the shepherds' god, and it remained the chief centre of his cult and of the pastoral music of which he was regarded as the inventor and patron.

ARETHUSA (X). The Nymph Arethusa is invoked by Virgil as a patroness of Sicilian pastoral poetry, though she began her career on the Greek mainland. The story is that, to escape her too ardent lover, the river-god Alpheus, she was turned into a fountain, which flowed under the Ionian Sea and reappeared as a spring in the island of Ortygia, at Syracuse, on the Sicilian coast. Shelley's poetry and the classical accomplishments of those responsible for the christening of H.M. warships have combined to keep her memory green.

ARGO (IV). The famous ship in which a picked band of adventurers (the Argonauts) were reputed to have set out in search of the Golden Fleece. The earliest mention of her is in Homer's *Odyssey*, Book XII, l. 70, where she is referred to as an already famous ship. The full story is told by Apollonius of Rhodes in his epic, the *Argonautica*.

ARION (VIII). The celebrated poet and player of the lyre. We are told that, on a voyage from Sicily to Corinth, he was attacked by the covetous crew for his wealth. Obtaining their leave to play one last piece before his death, he climbed to the bow of the ship and so charmed the gods and the music-loving dolphins by his song that when he leapt into the water the sea-beasts rallied to the rescue and carried him safely to land. Arion is a historical person, who lived about 600 B.C.

ARMENIAN (V). The reference to tigers as Armenian is not merely ornamental, for Bacchus and his cult were connected with the East. See also under *Bacchus*.

ASCRA (VI). A town in Boeotia where the Greek poet Hesiod lived.

ASSYRIA (III, IV). The name was used loosely for the country watered by the Rivers Euphrates and Tigris.

BACCHUS (V, VII). A Greek god (also known as Dionysus) concerned with the fertility of vegetation, in particular of the vine, and worshipped with orgiastic rites. His origin is obscure. Homer tells us very little about him, but one passage in the *Iliad* (VI, 130 ff.) certainly connects him with Thrace. In V Daphnis is credited with the distinction of having introduced his cult to the pastoral community.

BAVIUS (III). A contemporary poet who had shown himself hostile to Virgil.

BIANOR (IX). Servius tells us that Bianor was the founder of Mantua.

BRITONS (I). For Virgil's opinion of Britain and the Britons see the Essay on I.

CAESAR (IX). Caius Julius Caesar, the great Dictator, assassinated in 44 B.C. He is mentioned by name in IX only, but many scholars think that, under the disguise of Daphnis, Virgil is referring in V to his deification. See the Essay on that Eclogue.

CALLIOPE (IV). One of the Nine Muses, whose province was epic poetry. The legendary poet Orpheus was the son of Oeagrus and Calliope.

CERES (V). An Italian goddess of agriculture who was identified with the Greek Demeter. Her connection with corn led to the poetical use of her name for bread. Hence our 'cereal'.

CHALCIDIC (X). By 'Chalcidic verse' Virgil means poetry written in imitation, or in the style, of the Greek poet Euphorion of Chalcis, in Euboea. See Essay on X.

CHIAN (V). The Aegean island of Chios was noted for its wines.

CHROMIS (VI). A shepherd mentioned only in VI, where he takes part in the assault on Silenus.

CINNA (IX). Gaius Helvius Cinna, the author of an epic poem called *Smyrna*, which was admired by his friend Catullus and evidently by Virgil too. It has not survived. This is the 'Cinna the poet' of Shakespeare's *Julius Caesar*, III, 3 (see Essay on IX).

CIRCE (VIII). The witch encountered by Odysseus, as related in the tenth book of Homer's *Odyssey*.

CODRUS (V, VII). Figures in the title of a song in V, from which we can infer that he was of a quarrelsome disposition. In VII his poetry is highly praised by Corydon, and some scholars, including Servius, think that Virgil is referring to a contemporary poet.

CONON (III). A celebrated Greek mathematician and astronomer of the 3rd century B.C. The other scientist referred to but not named in the same passage in III is possibly Eudoxus, a pupil of Plato.

CORSICAN (IX). Corsican honey was noted for its bitterness; yews were considered bad for bees; and Virgil supposes yews to have been common in Corsica. Unless we have missed the point, the logic does not appear to be impeccable.

CORYDON (II, VII). A young shepherd. In II, of which he is the subject, he is in a subordinate position, Alexis being 'his master's' favourite. His claim to possess a thousand ewes must be taken as a boastful quotation from the Cyclops' song to Galatea in Theocritus (see H. J. Rose: *The Eclogues of Vergil*, Sather Classical Lectures,

1942; pp. 33–36). In VII he is the victor in a singing-match with Thyrsis.

CREMONA (IX). A town in Northern Italy founded as a Roman colony in 219 B.C. In the Civil Wars it sided against Octavian, who subsequently seized its lands for distribution among his veterans. It was not far from Mantua (Virgil's home town), which only partially escaped the same fate. See Essays on I and IX.

CRETAN (V, X). Crete was famous for its archery. In V we must presume Aegon to have been an immigrant from the island.

DAMOETAS (II, III, V). A countryman mentioned in II as having bequeathed his reed-pipe to Corydon on his deathbed. In III he is very much alive; he is the hired shepherd who, after an exchange of abuse, challenges Menalcas to a singing-match. Nevertheless, in V, we find Menalcas counting on him for a song at the Festival of Daphnis.

DAMON (III, VIII). In III he is referred to as a goat-owner who employs Tityrus and is defeated in a singing-match by Damoetas. In VIII he sings a love-song in competition with Alphesiboeus.

DAPHNIS (II, III, V, VII, VIII, IX). In II Daphnis is a good-looking country lad; in III he is a mere boy, who is bullied by Menalcas; but he figures in V as a deified hero (see Essay on that Eclogue). In VII he reappears as a shepherd who presides at a singing-match. In the witch-craft song in VIII he is the recalcitrant lover whom Amaryllis draws home from town by means of magic spells; and in IX he is a farmer who receives a piece of astronomical advice.

DELIAN (VII). Of Delos, a small island in the Aegean Sea, famous and sacred as the birthplace of Apollo and his sister Artemis, or Diana.

DODONA (IX). A place in Epirus celebrated for its oracle of Zeus. The god's utterances were detected in the whispering of the leaves in a grove of sacred oaks (see Homer's *Odyssey*, Book XIV, ll. 327–8.)

ETHIOPIAN (X). Virgil mentions Ethiopia as a typically hot country. It was one of the southernmost lands known to the Romans.

EUROTAS (VI). A river of Southern Greece, which rises in Arcadia and flows through Lacedaemon. Virgil is no doubt thinking of Apollo's love for the youth Hyacinthus, whom he courted on its banks.

FAUNS (V, VI). The Italian country-god Faunus was identified in literature with the Greek god Pan. His associate 'Fauns' thus became equivalent to the Satyrs who attended Pan.

GALATEA (I, III, VII, IX). In I she is a country girl who has discarded Tityrus. In III she is described affectionately as a saucy wench by Damoetas. In VII Corydon addresses her in a love-song as the daughter of Nereus, a sea-god – a promotion which shows that Virgil is thinking of her here as the legendary Galatea whom the Cyclops Polyphemus loved. This is certainly true in IX, where the little song addressed to her is derived from the famous and much longer appeal to his sea-love which Theocritus puts into Polyphemus' mouth.

GALLUS (VI, X). Gaius Cornelius Gallus, the poet and friend of Virgil. See the Essays on VI and X.

GARDENS OF THE WEST (VI). Trees bearing golden apples were a wedding present given by Earth to Zeus and Here. *Hesperides* is the name given both to the remote western islands where they grew and to the Nymphs who guarded them. It was with the help of these apples that Milanion succeeded in capturing the swift-footed maiden Atalanta (see Essay on VI).

GRYNEAN WOOD (VI). Grynium was a town on the coast of Asia Minor celebrated for a grove consecrated to Apollo, who had killed a serpent there. The point of the reference in VI is that the story was told by Euphorion of Chalcis, whose poems Gallus imitated (see Essay on X).

HEBRUS (X). The principal river of Thrace.

HERCULES (VII). The Latin name of Heracles, the hero of the Twelve Labours.

HESPER (X). Hesperus, the evening star.

HYBLAEAN (I, VII). Hybla was a town on the slopes of Mt Etna in Sicily, famous for its honey. Virgil's use of the adjective does not imply that he imagined Tityrus to have imported his bees or to take his naps on Etna. He uses it as a literary epithet in I, much as he uses it in VII of the wild-thyme which the bees of Hybla loved.

HYLAS (VI). A lad loved by Heracles, whom he accompanied in the ship *Argo* as far as the coast of Mysia. Landing there with the crew to find fresh water for the voyage, Hylas became separated from his friends. As he gazed down into a spring, the Naiads fell in love with his beauty and dragged him down into the water. The story is told by Apollonius of Rhodes in his *Argonautica* and by Theocritus.

HYLAX (VIII). The name of a watch-dog. It is Greek for 'barker'.

ILLYRIAN SEA (VIII). That part of the Adriatic which washes the shores of Dalmatia.

IOLLAS (II, III). A farmer, who in II may be presumed to be the master of Alexis, and in III is mentioned as one of the lovers of Phyllis.

ISMARUS (VI). A mountain in Thrace, the country of the Orpheus legend. The town of Ismarus is mentioned by Odysseus in the ninth book of the *Odyssey* as the scene of his encounter with the Cicones.

JOVE (III, IV). The supreme Olympian god (the Greek Zeus). The Latin nominative is Iuppiter, genitive Iovis; hence the English names, Jupiter and Jove.

LIBETHRUM (VII). A Thracian town near Mt Olympus. The district was sacred to the Muses.

LINUS (IV, VI). A legendary poet and singer, the son of Apollo, who was reputed, like Orpheus, to have caused the trees to move after him for love of his music.

LUCINA (IV). The goddess of childbirth, equated sometimes with Juno, but here with Diana, the sister of Phoebus Apollo.

LYCAEUS (X). A mountain in Arcadia, one of the centres of the cult of Pan.

LYCIDAS (VII, IX). In VII he is a handsome country lad admired by Thyrsis; in IX a shepherd-poet whom some scholars wish to identify with a member of Virgil's literary circle.

LYCŌRIS (X). The pseudonym used by Virgil for Gallus's mistress, the actress Cythĕris, and by Gallus himself in the poems he addressed to his love (see Essays on VI and X). The name and the pseudonym have, as usual, the same scansion.

MACEDONIAN (X). Virgil uses here the more localized term 'Sithonian'. Sithonia was the central peninsula of the three which jut out from Chalcidice in Macedonia.

MAENALUS (VIII, X). A mountain-range in Arcadia sacred to Pan.

MANTUA (IX). A small town standing on an island in the River Mincius, a tributary of the Po, in Northern Italy. It was the nearest market-town to the place of Virgil's birth. The fate of its territories under Octavian and his Commissioners is discussed in the Essays on I and IX.

MELIBOEUS (I, II, VII). In I a dispossessed farmer driven into exile. In II, if the same person is meant, he is still in possession of his flocks. He reappears in VII as the narrator of the singing-match at which Daphnis presides.

MENALCAS (II, III, V, IX, X). A countryman. In II he is the dusky but attractive youth with whom Corydon contrasts his favourite Alexis. In III he takes on Damoetas in a singing-match. In V he sings of the apotheosis of

Daphnis and incidentally claims to have composed II and III, or rather to have learnt them from the pipe which he presents to Mopsus. Even so, I do not think Virgil identifies Menalcas with himself, either in V or in IX, where he figures as a farmer-poet who has lost his land. In X, he reappears as one of the rustic swains who rally to the lovelorn Gallus, and cannot be the poet himself.

MEVIUS (III). A poet contemporary with Virgil, whose work he criticized unfavourably. Virgil retorts in III, and Horace called him 'stinking Mevius'. His poetry has not survived.

MICON (III, VII). A vineyard owner and a hunter.

MINCIUS (VII). The modern Mincio, a tributary of the River Po in Northern Italy. It flowed past Mantua, through Virgil's home country.

MNASYLLUS (VI). A shepherd mentioned only in VI, where he is associated with Chromis in the assault on Silenus.

MOERIS (VIII, IX). In the witchcraft song in VIII, Moeris is the champion wizard who supplies Amaryllis with her herbs and whose prowess in sorcery she handsomely acknowledges. But in IX he has turned into an elderly countryman who has lost his voice and forgotten most of the songs he used to sing as a boy.

MOPSUS (V, VIII). A young shepherd of peculiar tact and charm, who exchanges songs about Daphnis with Menalcas in V. In Damon's song in VIII, he is the future husband of the faithless Nysa.

MUSES (III, IV, VI-X). The Nine Muses, the 'choir of Phoebus', as Virgil calls them in VI, were the goddesses of poetry, music and literary composition in general. They are invoked or referred to in almost every Eclogue, sometimes as a body (Pierian Maidens, Nymphs of Libethrum, etc.), sometimes individually, as when Thalia is mentioned in VI, and Calliope in IV.

But as used by the Romans and ourselves, the word 'Muse' often means little more than poetry in general, or the poems or style of a particular author (e.g. 'my Muse' in III, and 'the Muse of Sophocles' in VIII). The 'Muses of Sicily' appealed to in IV are not another band of goddesses but a personification of the impulse that had inspired the pastoral poetry of Theocritus.

NAIADS (II, VI, X). Nymphs of fresh water (see under *Nymphs*). In X Virgil addresses them (perhaps because he has begun by invoking the fountain-nymph Arethusa) as though they were Muses, and complains of their indifference to the love-troubles of his friend, the poet Gallus. But it is quite likely that the Muses were themselves originally water-spirits.

NISUS (VI). See under *Scylla*.

NYMPHS (I, II, III, V, VI, VII, IX, X). 'Nymphs' is the general term for the personifications by which the fancy, or the perception, of the Greeks expressed the realities that they sensed in the phenomena of the countryside. The seas, the caves, the trees, the springs and lakes and rivers, all had their special kinds of Nymphs, of whom Virgil, in the *Eclogues*, mentions only the Naiads, or fresh-water spirits (II and VI), and the Dryads and Hamadryads, who lived in the trees (V and X).

It can be debated whether, to the average educated Roman, the Nymphs amounted to much more than a pretty conceit; but I argue in the Introduction that Virgil made a poet's use of the belief to embody a very genuine apprehension of reality.

NYSA (VIII). The faithless girl who jilts her lover to marry Mopsus in the song of Damon.

ODYSSEUS (VI, VIII). The wandering hero of Homer's *Odyssey* (Virgil uses the Latin name Ulysses, which is no longer favoured in English). The reference in VI is to Odysseus's disastrous passage between the rocky haunt of the monstrous Scylla and the whirlpool of Charybdis

(*Odyssey* XII); and in VIII to the transformation of his men into swine by the witch Circe (*Odyssey* X).

ORPHEUS (III, IV, VI, VIII). In Greek story, Thracian Orpheus figures as an early pre-Homeric poet and musician of fabulous skill. Son of the Muse Calliope, he sang so divinely to the harp that even trees and rocks were bewitched and followed him. In VI he is pictured as delighting the Thracian wilds with his music.

In post-Homeric times he was the centre of a number of mystical cults.

OXUS (I). An Asian river flowing into the Aral Sea.

PALAEMON (III). A countryman who judges the singing-match in III.

PALES (V). An Italian goddess (not taken over from Greek mythology), who presided over agricultural life.

PALLAS (II). Pallas Athene (the Roman Minerva) was not only the goddess of wisdom but the patroness of fortified cities, and of Athens in particular.

PAN (II, IV, V, VIII, X). The god of Arcadia, the patron of shepherds, protector of sheep, and inventor of the reed-pipe. His annoyance at finding unemployment among the reeds is described in VIII. In art he is depicted with horns on his forehead and the hind-legs of a goat. He figures thus on the famous Neptune Plate recently dug up at Mildenhall. In X Virgil pictures him, as he had seen his images, with face and brow stained red. This was a common practice – it is referred to in the description of the attack on Silenus in VI.

PARIS (II). The son of Priam, King of Troy, whose seduction of Helen, wife of Menelaus, led to the Trojan War. Virgil is thinking of his youth: he was brought up by the shepherds on Mt Ida.

PARNASSUS (VI, X). A mountain near Delphi in Greece, celebrated as one of the favourite haunts of Apollo and the Muses.

PARTHENIUS (X). A mountain in Arcadia, named, according to Servius, after the virgins who made it their hunting-ground.

PARTHIANS (I, X). The Parthians were successors to the Persian power in Mesopotamia and were for long Rome's most formidable enemies in the East. Their archers were famous, particularly for their skill in shooting behind them as they retreated – hence our 'Parthian shot'.

PASIPHAË (VI). The wife of Minos, King of Crete. The lady was indeed ill-starred. To punish her husband for a broken vow, the gods caused her to fall in love with a beautiful bull. The issue of this unhappy union was the Minotaur, a monstrous creature which was kept in the Labyrinth at Cnossus, till it was killed by Theseus, with the aid of Ariadne, its half-sister.

PERMESSUS (VI). A river descending from Mt Helicon in Boeotia, which was sacred to the Muses.

PHAETHON (VI). Phaethon was precocious enough to think himself capable of driving the fiery horses of his father, the Sun, and came to grief in the attempt. His sisters, who had abetted him in the adventure, mourned him so inconsolably that the gods in their pity turned them into trees (alders, here; in other versions, poplars).

PHILOMELA (VI). Philomela and Procne were daughters of Pandion, King of Athens. In the version of the story here followed by Virgil, Philomela was married to Tereus of Thrace and became the mother of Itylus. Tereus fell in love with his sister-in-law, Procne, violated her, and cut out her tongue to prevent her from denouncing him to his wife. She managed, however, to weave the information into a piece of cloth; and by way of revenge the sisters slew Itylus, served up his flesh to Tereus, and after the meal confronted him with his son's head. Then they fled, with Tereus in pursuit. All three were changed into birds, Tereus into a hoopoe, Procne into a swallow, and Philomela into a nightingale. In other versions of the tale, the names of the two ladies and of the birds they become are interchanged.

PHOEBUS APOLLO (III, IV, V, VI, VII, X). The son of Jove and Latona, and brother of Diana. He is the sun-god, and also the god of prophecy, of music and poetry, and of healing. In IV he is mentioned as the father of the poet Linus, and also in connection with the return of the Golden Age. In V we see him as the shepherds' patron – he had himself been made to serve a man, Admetus, as a shepherd. In VI, as the god of inspiration, he advises Virgil on his poetic career. In the same Eclogue his choir, the Muses, acclaim the poet Gallus. And again, in X, he reappears to remonstrate with his lovelorn devotee.

PHYLLIS (III, V, VII, X). A country girl, mentioned in III as beloved by Iollas and Damoetas. In V she figures in the title of a song. In VII, the farmer Meliboeus deplores the fact that he has no such servant-girl to help him with the lambs. In the same poem Thyrsis and Cory-don vie with each other in her praises. In X she is men-tioned once more as a typical country beauty, whom Gallus would be glad to accept in exchange for his sophisticated actress friend.

PIERIAN (VI, VIII, X). Pieria was a district in the neigh-bourhood of Mt Olympus in Greece, connected from early times with the cult of the Muses, who are often referred to as Pierian goddesses.

PINDUS (X). A range of mountains in Northern Greece. It was one of the traditional haunts of the Muses, whose functions the Naiads appear to be usurping in X, where Virgil disposes of their possible alibi on Pindus.

POLLIO (III, IV). Gaius Asinius Pollio, the poet, historian and politician, and friend of Virgil. He was Consul in 40 B.C. (see Essay on IV) and played a leading part in the reconciliation of Octavian and Antony that was effected in that year and forms the background of Virgil's prophecy of a peaceful age. His poetry is mentioned in

III and again in VIII, which appears to be dedicated to him. His works are lost.

PONTUS (VIII). A country in Asia Minor on the south coast of the Black Sea. It was the proverbial home of poisons and of poisoners.

PRIAPUS (VII). A minor deity, one of whose special functions was the protection of gardens.

PROETUS (VI). A king of Argos whose three daughters boasted that they were more beautiful than the goddess Here, and were punished by being made to imagine that they were cows. In the end they were cured of this delusion by the seer Melampus.

PROMETHEUS (VI). Originally a fire-god, Prometheus figures in Greek legend as the Titan who stole fire from heaven to give it to mankind, and was punished for his enterprise by Zeus. He was chained to a rock on Mt Caucasus, and his liver was pecked at by an eagle and perpetually renewed.

PYRRHA (VI). The wife of Deucalion, who, with her husband, is said to have created mankind, or created them afresh after the Flood, by throwing stones behind her back at the gods' command.

RHINE (X). Virgil dismisses the much-lauded river as typical of the back of beyond, and cold into the bargain. From the time of Julius Caesar it was the frontier river between Roman territory and the wilds of Germany.

RHODOPE (VI, VIII). A range of high mountains in Thrace, the country of the Orpheus legend.

ROME (I). The capital city of Italy. In I, its size and splendour are contrasted by a simple rustic visitor with the insignificance of his own market-town, the name of which is not given.

SARDINIAN (VII). The plant referred to is a kind of Ranunculus, the English celery-leaved crowfoot. Its bitterness is said to have given rise to the expression 'sardonic smile'.

SATURN (IV, VI). A god of agriculture in early Italian mythology. Later he was identified with the Greek Cronos, who was dethroned by his son Zeus. His name is connected with a time when the earth enjoyed a Golden Age.

SCYLLA (VI). There were two creatures of this name, whom Virgil and other Roman poets appear to have confused. The monster described here is obviously the Scylla whom Odysseus encountered on his travels (*Odyssey*, XII); but this Scylla was the daughter of Phorcys and Cratais. Scylla the daughter of Nisus suffered a more complete but less revolting transformation and became a bird.

SCYTHIA (I). The wild and remote region which we know as southern Russia.

SIBYLLINE (IV). See Essay on IV.

SICILIAN (II, IV, VI, X). In the introductory lines of IV and VI Virgil uses the name by way of acknowledging his indebtedness to Theocritus, the pastoral poet who laid the scene of many of his Idyls in Sicily. In X the reference is to the story of Arethusa the Syracusan Nymph (see under *Arethusa*).

SILENUS (VI). See Essay on VI.

SILVANUS (X). An Italian woodland deity.

SOPHOCLES (VIII). The great Athenian dramatist (496–406 B.C.).

STIMICHON (V). A shepherd mentioned in V as an appreciative critic of music.

TEREUS (VI). See under *Philomela*.

THALIA (VI). The Muse of pastoral poetry and of comedy.

THESTYLIS (II). A country wench who is represented in II as waiting on the reapers.

THYRSIS (VII). The defeated contestant in the singing-match with Corydon, where they are described as 'Arcadians both'.

Timavus (VIII). A river in north-eastern Italy, forming the boundary between Venetia and Istria.

Tiphys (IV). The helmsman of the famous *Argo* in the expedition in search of the Golden Fleece.

Tityrus (I, III, VI, VIII, IX). In I he is an elderly countryman who has saved his farm from seizure, and incidentally purchased his freedom, by a timely journey to Rome and application to the highest authorities. In III he is mentioned as a goatherd looking after Damon's flocks. In VI his name is playfully used by Apollo in addressing Virgil himself as a pastoral poet – our only real justification for identifying Virgil with Tityrus. In VIII he is referred to as a typical shepherd-musician, and in IX is once more told to look after someone else's goats.

Tmaros (VIII). A mountain in Epirus.

Varius (IX). Lucius Varius Rufus, a distinguished poet of the Augustan age, who won the friendship of Virgil, Horace and Maecenas. His works have not survived. See also Essay on IX.

Varus (VI, IX). The Varus to whom Virgil addresses VI and whom he mentions in IX as the recipient of the poetical appeal on behalf of the Mantuan lands is usually identified with Publius Alfenus Varus. Servius tells us that this same Varus had studied philosophy with Virgil under Siro the Epicurean and that he was one of the commissioners appointed to allot lands to veterans in Northern Italy. The identification is doubtful.

Venus (VII). The goddess of Love (Greek Aphrodite).

Vesper (VI). The evening or the evening star.

Also translated by E. V. Rieu,
editor of the Penguin Classics:

THE ODYSSEY OF HOMER

SOME PRESS OPINIONS:

'I had forgotten how easy it was for the Greekless reader to enjoy the two epics, "The Wrath of Achilles" and "The Return of Odysseus", until Mr. Rieu's translation of "The Odyssey" reminded me.' ... Desmond McCarthy in the *Sunday Times*.

'Mr Rieu translates actively and sensitively what is arguably the best story in the world into a prose that is lucid and rapid and has sufficient dignity to sustain the narrative. ... On the whole he catches the directness and simplicity and poise of the original better than any previous translator. ... The book is more pleasant to read and to handle than many at ten times its price.' – *Listener*.

'A new translation in which Homer's words are still winged, though English, and no attempt is made to insist that the prose of translation need be prosaic.' – *Tribune*.

'... the homespun humour and deft characterisation of the humbler characters lose nothing by the racy English of Mr Rieu's rendering. ... The proof of the pudding lies in the eating, and this one is, beyond question, being eagerly devoured – a fact easily verified by anyone who travels by bus or train, and supported by the enthusiastic testimony of one's own friends.' – *Time and Tide*.

'Mr Rieu has achieved a compromise, admirably adapted to commend to the Greekless novel-reader of to-day on this side of the Atlantic, this eternally fresh story from the youth of the world.' – *Times Literary Supplement*.

'In the world of books something important has happened – more interesting than the publication of a shelf full of best sellers. There is a new translation of the Odyssey, a very contemporary translation, and it costs only one shilling. This is revolutionary. ... It is the Odyssey very much as a novel, still with all the oceanic surge but without some of the thunder. Almost colloquial, but sinewy and of our own experience.' – *Reynolds' News*.